JUSTIFICATION AND EMANCIPATION

T0326939

PENN STATE SERIES IN CRITICAL THEORY

Eduardo Mendieta, General Editor

The Penn State Series in Critical Theory showcases the work
of contemporary critical theorists who are building upon and
expanding the canon of the Frankfurt School. Based on a series of
symposia held at Penn State University, each volume in the series
contains an original essay by an internationally renowned critical
theorist, followed by a set of critical essays from a number of
authors as well as the theorist's response to these essays. Books in
the series will focus especially on topics that have been previously
neglected by the Frankfurt tradition, including colonialism and
imperialism, racism, sexism, and ethnocentrism. They offer
analyses and readings that show the continuing relevance of one
of the most innovative intellectual traditions of the last century.

Also in the series:

Amy Allen and Eduardo Mendieta, eds., *From Alienation to Forms of Life:
The Critical Theory of Rahel Jaeggi*

Justification and Emancipation

The Critical Theory of Rainer Forst

EDITED BY AMY ALLEN AND EDUARDO MENDIETA

The Pennsylvania State University Press
University Park, Pennsylvania

Library of Congress Cataloging-in-Publication Data

Names: Allen, Amy, 1970– editor. | Mendieta,
    Eduardo, editor.
Title: Justification and emancipation : the critical
    theory of Rainer Forst / edited by Amy Allen and
    Eduardo Mendieta.
Other titles: Penn State series in critical theory.
Description: University Park, Pennsylvania : The
    Pennsylvania State University Press, [2019] |
    Series: Penn State series in critical theory |
    Includes bibliographical references and index.
Summary: "A collection of essays on the work of
    German political theorist Rainer Forst, covering
    subjects such as justice, toleration, and the critique
    of power from within a normative theory of justice
    and law"—Provided by publisher.
Identifiers: LCCN 2019028819 | ISBN 9780271084787
    (paperback)
Subjects: LCSH: Forst, Rainer, 1964– | Critical theory.
    | Justification (Ethics) | Justice (Philosophy)
Classification: LCC HM480.J89 2019 | DDC 142—dc23
LC record available at https://lccn.loc.gov/2019028819

The Pennsylvania State University Press is a member
of the Association of University Presses.

It is the policy of The Pennsylvania State University
Press to use acid-free paper. Publications on uncoated
stock satisfy the minimum requirements of American
National Standard for Information Sciences—
Permanence of Paper for Printed Library Material,
ANSI Z39.48-1992.

CONTENTS

CONTENTS

ACKNOWLEDGMENTS

First and foremost, we want to express our deep gratitude to Rainer Forst for agreeing to have his work meet the scholarly scrutiny of some exacting and original thinkers and for his generosity and determination to see this book into press through some busy and challenging times. We must also thank all our symposium participants for their superior contributions. The symposium that gave birth to this volume was generously supported by the following units at Penn State: the Department of Philosophy, the Rock Ethics Institute, the Institute for Arts and Humanities (now the Humanities Institute), the Department of Germanic and Slavic Languages and Literatures, and the School of Global Languages, Literatures, and Cultures. We are grateful for their generous support and their assistance in promoting the symposium. We are especially thankful to Pablo Gilabert and Mattias Iser, who served as commentators for the symposium; Mattias subsequently agreed to contribute a paper written especially for this volume. We also wish to thank our Penn State University graduate students who chaired and moderated the symposium sessions: Kristopher Klotz and Nicole Yokum. Filipe Campello, of the Federal University of Pernambuco in Recife, Brazil, a Fulbright Visiting Fellow at the New School, also chaired one of our sessions. We had amazing logistical support from Emily Slimak, who coordinated travel, hotel, and meal arrangements. Finally, we want to thank Kendra Boileau, our editor at Penn State University Press, for her enthusiasm, support, and patience. We are excited to see this next stage of our productive partnership come to fruition.

Amy Allen and Eduardo Mendieta
STATE COLLEGE, PENNSYLVANIA
JANUARY 2019

CHAPTER 1

Introduction

Amy Allen and Eduardo Mendieta

1. RAINER FORST'S WORK IN CONTEXT

The Institute for Social Research in Frankfurt am Main, which would become the institutional home for the "Frankfurt School" of critical theory, was officially established on February 3, 1923,[1] making it now nearly one hundred years old. The first director was Carl Grünberg, an avowed Marxist, whom some considered the father of "Austro-Marxism." Due to health reasons, however, the directorship of the institute soon passed to Max Horkheimer, who, over a series of important essays published in the 1930s, laid out the institute's research agenda. Thus if one considers Horkheimer's 1931 "The Present Situation in Social Philosophy and the Tasks of an Institute for Social Research,"[2] the classic 1937 "Traditional and Critical Theory" (unquestionably the most emblematic and forward-looking of his essays), and the latter's "Postscript,"[3] one can note already several characteristics that mark out the distinctive methodology of the Frankfurt School: the engagement with contemporary thinkers as manifesting trends in contemporary society; a critical stance toward both positivist empiricism and speculative metaphysics; an explicitly Marxist analysis of the social conditions of classes and individuals; a focus on culture, whether it be high- or so-called low-brow culture, ranging from music and painting to literature and theater; and finally, an avowed commitment that the research on the present social and psychological conditions of society was undertaken with an interest in transformation. As he put it in his 1937 essay, "[But] a critical theory of society as it is, a theory dominated at every turn by a concern for reasonable conditions of life."[4] In the "Postscript" to the essay, Horkheimer's language is less Aesopian. He writes, "However extensive the interaction between critical theory and the special sciences whose progress the theory must respect and on which it has for decades exercised a liberating and stimulating influence, the theory never aims simply at an increase in knowledge. Its goal is man's emancipation from slavery."[5] The aim of critical theory, then, is not simply the scholastic accumulation of data but rather the transformation of both the social critic and the society to which she belongs. Critical theory is oriented toward a form of societal emancipation that, first, turns blind necessity into meaningful necessity and, second, gives all individuals an "equal chance of self-development."[6] To quote a now-famous slogan, critical theory holds fast to the idea that "Another World Is Possible," one in which justice can be achieved.

In the early 1980s, Jürgen Habermas sought to reground and redefine the research agenda of the "Frankfurt School." At the end of his magnum opus, *The Theory of Communicative Action,* in the chapter titled "The Tasks of Critical Theory," Habermas notes that the work of the Institute for Social Research had been dominated by six themes: (1) the question of the sociopsychological integration of individuals in postliberal societies, (2) ego development and family socialization, (3) the emergence of mass media and the creation of mass culture, (4) research into the "authoritarian personality" and the "cessation" of social and political protest, (5) the development of an aesthetic theory that would take into account the seismic shift in both the means of production and social consumption of art, and finally (6) the hallmark of critical theory—the criticism of positivism, empiricism, and their attendant technocracy.[7]

Habermas then proceeds to show how these same—or very similar—research agendas can and should be undertaken within the framework of the theory of communicative action, which, among other things, has dispensed with a Marxist-inflected philosophy of history and the philosophy of consciousness, or the philosophy of the Cartesian, Kantian, solitary, and unburdened cognitive subject. As Habermas put it, "The theory of communicative action is meant to provide an alternative to the philosophy of history on which earlier critical theory still relied, but which is no longer tenable. It is intended as a framework within which interdisciplinary research on the selective pattern of capitalist modernization can be taken up once again."[8] It is noteworthy that Habermas ends his massive *The Theory of Communicative Action* with a gloss on Marx's methodological introduction to his 1857 *Critique of Political Economy,* specifically a gloss on the argument why political economy departed from the basic assumption of a "seemingly simple abstraction"—namely, labor. Habermas then writes, "As I have argued above, when labor is rendered abstract and indifferent, we have a special case of the transference of communicatively structured domains of action over to the media-steered interaction. This interpretation decodes the deformation of the lifeworld with the help of another category, namely, 'communicative action.'"[9] Marx had argued in his introduction to his critique of political economy that even the most abstract of categories, which may be valid for all other stages of social development, in their very character as abstractions are likewise products of specific historical relations. Habermas takes this to mean not that theory is simply diagnostic of societal crises but that in its abstractness, it reflects the very society that gave their conscious expression. This means that theory is the making conscious of the very social dynamics that gave rise to the abstraction. As Habermas put it, "The theory of communicative action can explain why this is so: the development of society must *itself* give rise to the problem situations that *objectively* afford contemporaries a privileged access to the general structure of the lifeworld."[10] While critical theory, now in the form of a theory of communicative action, may look backward, insofar as it works closely with the reconstructive social sciences, it also looks forward to social transformation and emancipation—that is, to releasing the emancipatory contents embedded in the lifeworld that is both the background for and the product of communicative interaction.

Still, like Horkheimer and all other members of the Institute for Social Research, Habermas's work is also marked by a distinct modus

JUSTIFICATION AND EMANCIPATION

operandi—namely, the immanent critique of other theories and thinkers. If the aim is to pluck the rose from the chains of theoretical reification, then this calls for a relentless immanent engagement with extant theories. The elucidation of the normative contents embedded in the lifeworld through the reconstructions provided by the social sciences goes hand in hand with an ongoing reconstruction of social theory and philosophy itself. This important aspect of critical theory cannot be underscored enough.

The observation allows us to make the following claim about critical theory by way of an image implanted in the Western philosophical imaginary by Paul Ricoeur. In his magisterial interpretation of Freud, Ricoeur reads the founder of psychoanalysis not merely as a psychologist or physician but rather as a philosopher of interpretation and hermeneutics. In order to advance this thesis, Ricoeur places Freud alongside Marx and Nietzsche and coins the term *masters of suspicion* to characterize these towering figures. If hermeneutics begins with them, then the task of interpretation "is no longer to spell out the consciousness of meaning, but to *decipher its expressions*."[11] For the three masters of suspicion, the fundamental category is the relation "hidden-shown, or simulated-manifest."[12] The key passage, however, is the following: "Fundamentally, the *Genealogy of Morals* in Nietzsche's sense, the theory of ideologies in the Marxist sense, and the theory of ideals and illusions in Freud's sense represent three convergent procedures of demystification."[13] Ricoeur's insight and naming of these masters of suspicion allow us to recognize that there is no consciousness without critical reflection—that is, without suspicion. Freud liked to speak of the three great demotions in the history of thought: the Copernican revolution, which displaced humans from the center of the cosmos; the Darwinian revolution, which destroyed the great chain of being, turning the human into just another living creature that has evolved bereft of God and divine providence; and finally, the Freudian revolution, which displaced the transparent, sovereign Cartesian and Kantian ego from the court of reason by revealing the extent to which our motives and justifications are not transparent to us. According to Ricoeur, however, the three masters of suspicion can be seen as affirming the power of reason to cut through the tangle of false consciousness, guilty moral consciousness, and neurosis.

If we thus think of Marx, Nietzsche, and Freud not as the priests of false and deluded consciousness but as masters of suspicion working in the service of the self-clarification of consciousness by means of the critique of what is "hidden-shown, or simulated-manifest," we can then begin to appreciate how we can place them next to another, perhaps somewhat unlikely, master of suspicion—namely, Immanuel Kant. Now, Kant's work, notwithstanding its translucent systematicity, is suffused by metaphors and allegories, as Michèle Le Doeuff showed in her still indispensable *The Philosophical Imaginary*[14] and Willi Goetschel has documented exhaustively in *Constituting Critique: Kant's Writing as Critical Praxis*.[15] From among the many metaphors present in Kant's corpus, one is essential to the claim that Kant can be read not as a defender of the sovereignty of reason but rather as a master of suspicion: reason as a tribunal (*Gerichtshof*).[16] The passage where Kant deploys this metaphor is to be found in the preface to the first edition of the first critique, and it reads, "This is evidently the effect not of the thoughtlessness of our age, but of its ripened *power of judgment*, which will no longer be put off with illusory knowledge, and which demands that reason should take on anew the most difficult of all its tasks, namely, that of self-knowledge, and to institute a court of justice, by which reason may secure its rightful claims while dismissing all its groundless pretensions, and this not by mere decrees but according to its own eternal and unchangeable laws; and this court is none other than the *critique of pure reason* itself."[17] By figuring reason as a tribunal, Kant abandons the metaphysical conception of reason as something whose function is to ground claims about the world. Instead, at the core of this judicial metaphor is the notion that rather than grounding or proving, reason legitimates—that is, provides justifications.[18] As Onora O'Neill proposed, "*Justification* or *vindication* of reason, rather than *proof* or *foundation* for reason. Justification differs from proof in that it is directed to some audience, and unconditional justification must be directed to audiences without assuming that they meet any specific conditions, so must be directed to all agents. . . . Kant calls it *public* or *autonomous* reasoning."[19] By shifting from the conception of reason as a monolithic, stable, and transcendent ground to a conception of reason as *justificatory* and *vindicating,* reason becomes both procedural and public: reason as a process of providing and redeeming justifications must be performed within a public "space of reasons." If reason's performance is vindicatory and justificatory, then, as Martin Jay put it succinctly and provocatively, "not only was there a 'space of reasons,' to invoke the American philosopher Wilfrid Sellars's celebrated phrase, but also a 'time of reasons,' in which rationality was understood as involving intersubjective deliberation, argumentation, adjudication and education."[20] The "space of reasons" is, as O'Neill notes, quintessentially a "public space"—that is, always open, nonexclusive, and nonhierarchical. However, as Jay notes, the "time of reasons" also entails, first, that there is a time when justifications—reasons—must be proffered and, second, that the way we think of what counts as reasons and the grounds on which those reasons are either acceptable or unacceptable remain fundamentally open to change and transformation.

No one has elevated the practice of *critique* to a higher pedestal than Kant.[21] It may be hyperbolic to claim that there would be no Nietzsche, Marx, or Freud without Kant—the Kant of reason as critique. It is in this sense that we should see him also as a master of suspicion, in light of Ricoeur and articulated eloquently by Goetschel, who wrote, "If the term *critique,* before Kant, denoted the philosophical task of restoring a text in order to establish its authenticity, Kant has redefined it as complex, self-reflective, epistemological procedure for constructing knowledge. As a result, authenticity is replaced by the transcendental method of critique. Knowledge has to legitimate itself from now on as a self-constituting process. Reason assumes the place of the judge, critique represents the court, and the *Critique of Pure Reason* serves as the record of the trial."[22] If we think of critical theory as a research agenda that focuses on contemporary society, as a distinct tradition built from a relentless engagement with certain classics, and above all as the quest to give an account that rescues reason from the thorny bush of damaged life and alienated social existence, we cannot fail to notice the centrality of Nietzsche, Marx, Freud, and Kant. There is no thinker within the critical theory tradition that has returned to Kant as a master of suspicion—a thinker of reason as critique and thus as the practice of justification and vindication—as generatively as Rainer Forst.

2. KEY WORKS AND CONCEPTS

Rainer Forst is presently a professor of political theory and philosophy at the Goethe University in Frankfurt. He is the founding codirector of the interdisciplinary cluster, the Formation of Normative Orders, which is affiliated with Goethe University. In 2012, he received the Gottfried Leibniz Prize, the most prestigious award for German researchers.

Forst made a prominent entry into the philosophical world with the 1994 publication of his sweeping but also painstakingly researched *Contexts of Justice: Political Philosophy beyond Liberalism and Communitarianism.* Forst's text was a much-needed intervention in the heated debate between liberal political philosophers and communitarians that raged during the 1980s and early 1990s. Appropriating a metaphor from Seyla Benhabib, Forst argued that persons, conceived in the most general sense, are "situated" members of distinct and plural communities. To be situated within these communities means above all that persons are recognized as both authors and addressees of justifications that are proffered within the different normative orders within which we find ourselves situated. Forst distinguished among *four* normative contexts in which persons find themselves embedded as both creators and vindicators of justifications: First, there are ethical contexts in which we are socialized into certain communal bonds and obligations. Second, there are legal contexts that aim to provide a legal abode to the "ethical identity" of consociates that de jure and de facto recognize them as authors and enactors of the law—that is, subjects of the law and legal persons. Third, there are political contexts in which individuals are recognized as active creators of legislation that lead to the juridification of legal equality and liberty. Fourth, there is the context of the moral community of all human beings who have an equal right to moral respect. As Forst claims, partly giving us the key to his theory, "A *theory* of justice is at the same time context-bound and context-transcending insofar as it takes these normative dimensions into consideration, without absolutizing any particular one. According to this theory, the *society* that unites these contexts in the appropriate manner can be called just."[23] *Contexts of Justice* is truly a work of encyclopedic synthesis that develops a theory of justice via an immanent critique of liberal and communitarian political theories. Forst's next book, guided by the same modus operandi of theoretical reconstruction and synthesis, is *Toleration in Conflict: Past and Present*.[24] In this massive work, Forst constructs a historical narrative of the different discourses on toleration, beginning in antiquity; going through the Middle Ages, the Reformation, and the Peace of Westphalia; and culminating in our contemporary debates about what can and can't be tolerated. Without question, Forst's is the most comprehensive history of the concept and practice of toleration. Yet it is also a systematic work, one that aims to articulate the normative grounds of toleration. Here historical reconstruction and *Begriffsgeschichte* have a systemic and normative intent insofar as they reveal the structure of toleration by interrogating the ways that it is invariably embedded in contexts in which power is being curbed, deployed, or legitimated by "moral" claims.

In *Toleration in Conflict*, Forst distinguishes among four conceptions of toleration, each one making explicit both the claims of power and the claims of reason and morality. According to the first, the *permission conception*, toleration is a relation between an authority and some group or persons who are granted some modicum of accommodation but not acceptance: "Toleration here means that the authority (or majority) grants the minority the permission to live in accordance with its conviction so long as it—and this is the crucial condition—does not question the predominance of the authority (or majority)."[25] Forst adduces the 1598 Edict of Nantes as a historical exemplar of this conception.

The second, the *coexistence conception* of toleration, resembles the first insofar as its goal is the avoidance of conflict. Under this conception, toleration is advocated on instrumental and pragmatic terms. The difference from the permission conception, however, is that according to the coexistence conception, rival groups relate to each other as equally powerful, or potentially as being able to push or advocate with the same strength their interests, leading to a stalemate. Here it may be said that the relationship of accommodation among groups is not horizontal but vertical.[26]

The third, the *respect conception,* stands in stark contrast to the prior two. Under this conception, toleration follows from a morally justified *respect* for individuals and groups. As Forst puts it, "The tolerating parties respect one another as autonomous persons or as equally entitled members of a political community constituted under the rule of law."[27] The respect conception, which is also the one that Forst defends, is based on the respect of the moral autonomy of individuals and the consequent "right to justification" of moral and legal norms that can claim to be reciprocally and generally valid.

The fourth, the *esteem conception* of toleration, with historical roots in Renaissance humanism and forms of romanticism, appears as the most recent because of efforts to juridify and enact it in policies affecting multicultural societies. This conception has emerged in the last half-century through debates and discussions about the relationship between multiculturalism and toleration. Under this conception, toleration calls for a more robust form of mutual recognition than the one found in the respect conception. Here toleration is not simply respect but the affirmation and esteem of the convictions and practices of individuals or groups that are furthermore seen as ethically valuable to the entire community—and not merely to those who espouse those unique practices and values. On this understanding, multiculturalism is not a modus vivendi but an affirmation of ethical pluralism that is understood as a valuable asset to the community as a whole.

Forst's aim in identifying these four conceptions of toleration, however, is to show that toleration is a "normatively dependent concept." By reconstructing the history and evolution of toleration, Forst argues, we can clearly see it as a practice of justification that is guided by three elements: objection, acceptance, and rejection. In other words, toleration means that objections, acceptance, and ultimate rejection of a certain practice be "justified" by reasons that are mutually and generally accepted, reasons that furthermore ought to be equally acceptable to all. As Forst would put it in a later dialogue with political philosopher Wendy Brown, "The art of toleration is an art of finding proper reasons that can be presented to others when you think that they should

9

conform to a norm that they don't agree with in their practices and beliefs. *It consists in distinguishing your reasons for objection from mutually justifiable reasons for rejection.* The latter have a higher threshold of justification."[28] In 2007, Forst published *Das Recht auf Rechtfertigung: Elemente einer Konstruktivitischen Theorie der Gerechtkeit.*[29] It bears registering the German title, which would be cumbersome to translate literally, as either *Right from Justification* or *Right on Justification,* but both would sound rather jarring in English. The official English translation is *The Right to Justification: Elements of a Constructivist Theory of Justice.*[30] The linguistic point that we are trying to make is that in German, at the very least, *Recht,* which means both "law" and "right," is linked to justification (*Rechtfertigung*) and that justification somehow leads to the recognition of right and/or law. Forst begins with the unsuspecting but brilliant recognition that the various ways in which human beings have been defined by political philosophy since its inception with the Greeks in Athens, including *animal rationale, zoon logikon* and *zoon politikon,* really sketch an image of the human being as a *justificatory being.* The human being is a creature that always gives reasons and always expects them. Human beings are also creatures of praxis, of intersubjective practical action that takes place in the context of a community. To this extent, humans are also creatures that inescapably and relentlessly find themselves embedded within "orders of justification." The political realm, then, is an order of justification. As *justificatory beings,* we are, as it were, always dwelling in the *noumenal* realm of the space of reasons and the time of reason, to use Jay's most apropos expression. Within the political order, however, the most important normative concept is that of justice, understood not as the distribution of goods but rather as the creation of the appropriate orders of justification in which individual's claims can be heard, respected, and adjudicated. In fact, Forst has articulated a forceful critique of a distributive conception that views justice as a mathematical calculus of the distribution of goods to citizens. This is a picture of justice that holds us captive and, in so doing, obscures substantive questions about the relations of domination and oppression under which such goods are produced and distributed.

According to Forst, there is another picture of justice that has yet to captivate our collective imaginary. This picture begins from the negative experience of injustice. Injustice is experienced and institutionalized when power is wielded and deployed arbitrarily, when the concerns of citizens are neither acknowledged nor addressed. In this alternate picture, justice is first and foremost a matter of the justifiability of certain social relations, grounded in the recognition of the essential intersubjective relationality of justificatory beings. When we are liberated from the calculative conception of justice as a distribution of goods, we are able to consider "the *first question of justice*—the justifiability of social relations and the distribution of the 'power of justification' within a political context" and only then "is a radical conception of justice possible: one that gets to the roots of social injustice. This insight is at the center of a *critical theory of justice,* whose first 'good' is the socially effective power to demand, question, or provide justifications, and to turn them into the foundations of political action and institutional arrangements."[31] The keystone, then, of Rainer Forst's constructivist theory of justice is the "right to justification."

From this overview of Forst's major works, certain key concepts have emerged: Forst's particular brand of contextualist or situated universalism, his historically rich but ultimately normatively dependent conception of toleration, and the right to justification as the core of his reconceptualization of justice. In his more recent work, two further concepts have come to the fore that enrich and expand his critical theory, both of which play a central role in the discussions in this volume: progress and noumenal power.

Like toleration, Forst views progress as a normatively dependent concept, one that is indexed to the basic moral and human right that is the right to justification.[32] And yet he also defends progress as an essential concept for critical theory, one that is necessarily invoked in any project of critique: to criticize an institution, practice, or political structure as unjust is to presuppose that it would be better if things were otherwise; thus all forms of critique, even postcolonial critiques of the ideology of progress, are implicitly committed to progress in some sense of the term. This means that progress is a reflexive concept. As Forst explains, "Every progressive process must be constantly questioned as to whether it is in the social interest—correctly understood—of those who are part of this process. Thus, every criticism is itself also part of progress."[33] Hence even as Forst agrees that we must acknowledge and reject the ideological misuses of the concept of progress, he insists that critical theory cannot do without it. The key is to disentangle the concept of progress from the logics of colonial domination, in which it has all too often been embedded, precisely by emphasizing that it is up to those affected by historical developments to decide whether they count as progress or not. Thus in Forst's view, self-determination is central to progress.[34]

With the notion of noumenal power, Forst extends his account of the space of reasons as an order of justifications into a conceptualization of power relations.[35] Noumenal power consists first and foremost of the ability of some to close off or structure the space of reasons for another, thus producing ideological justifications (of which the ideological notion of progress is a prominent example). The core idea of this conception of power is that, unlike physical violence, power necessarily operates through the mediation of reasons. "To be a subject of power," Forst writes, "is to be moved by reasons that others have given me and that motivate me to think or act in a certain way intended by the reason-giver."[36] If human beings are fundamentally justificatory beings, beings who give and expect justifications, then power relations among human beings will necessarily take the form of justifications, which can be good or bad, legitimate or ideological, emancipatory or oppressive. The job of critique, in this conception, is to submit justificatory narratives to the tribunal of reason in order to distinguish the ideological and oppressive justifications from the legitimate and emancipatory ones: to develop, in other words, a critical theory of relations of justification. As Forst puts it, "Critique aims specifically at false, or at least one-sided, justifications for asymmetrical social relations that fall short of the criteria of reciprocity and generality, in short, relations of domination."[37] Thus just as for the early Frankfurt School, the ultimate aim of Forst's critical theory of justification is emancipation.

3. OVERVIEW OF THE VOLUME

The relationships among power, domination, progress, and justificatory reason are central to the opening chapter of this volume, Rainer Forst's essay "The Justification of Progress and the Progress of Justification."

Forst further develops his conception of progress, defending it against the line of critique frequently advanced in postcolonial theory (recently articulated in relation to Frankfurt School critical theory by Amy Allen).[38] Rejecting both Hegelian historicism and radical genealogical contextualism as conventionalist and self-undermining, respectively, Forst offers a vigorous defense of context-transcending notions of progress and reason as central to all forms of critique, including postcolonial ones.

The next six chapters of this volume take up various themes in Forst's work. John Christman's "Autonomy and Justification: What Reasons Do We Owe Each Other and Ourselves?" explores the mutually implicating demands of personal autonomy and interpersonal justification. In Christman's analysis, social and political practices of justification must be acceptable to participants in those practices from the point of view of their practical identities, or else a wedge is driven between justice and autonomy. Christman argues that conditions of social oppression, exclusion, and violence, by undermining participants' trust in social and political institutions, can thus alienate them from public practices of justification. These conditions thus pose unresolved—and perhaps unresolvable—challenges for Forst's conception of justice as justification. Mattias Iser, in his "Objectionable Objections: On Toleration, Respect, and Esteem," critically analyzes Forst's defense of the respect conception of tolerance, arguing that this conception allows for too many objectionable objections—that is, objections on the part of majority cultures to the practices of minority groups that are harmful even if they do not directly violate conditions of mutual respect. Iser argues that in order to address this problem, Forst's respect conception needs to be supplemented with an esteem condition that Forst himself explicitly rejects but that Iser thinks is implicit in the right to justification. Catherine Lu's essay, "The Right to Justification and the Good of Nonalienation," considers conflicts that arise between actually existing orders of justification, especially in (post)colonial contexts. Echoing a point made by John Christman, Lu reminds us that in such contexts, public practices of justification may be experienced as alienating to indigenous or formerly colonized subjects. In order to deal with this problem, Lu suggests that Forst needs a richer conception of nonalienation that encompasses its ethical and existential

13

dimensions. John McCormick's chapter, "'A Certain Relation in the Space of Justifications,'" explores Forst's conception of noumenal power. McCormick argues that although this conception has distinct advantages over realist conceptions of power, it is also prone to certain ambiguities concerning intentionality and the relationship between thought and action. He also draws on the work of Machiavelli and Foucault to question Forst's claim for the comprehensiveness of his account of noumenal power. Without denying the importance of noumenal power, McCormick contends that nonreason-giving, objectivizing forms of power also play a necessary role in politics. In her contribution, "Opening 'Political Contexts of Injustice,'" Melissa Yates argues that Forst's work challenges us to open what count as contexts of injustice in laudable ways, especially through his analysis of multiple forms of domination that crosscut transnational contexts. However, she also suggests two ways in which Forst's work may not be quite open enough, both because it lacks an account of transtemporal contexts of injustice and because the right to justification may be too narrow to effectively make space for genuinely new, unfamiliar, or foreign participants and their claims. Finally, Sarah Clark Miller's "A Feminist Engagement with Forst's Transnational Justice" assesses the strengths and weaknesses of Forst's conception of justice through the lens of transnational feminist theory, with an emphasis on gender-based sexual violence. Miller identifies promising synergies between Forst's theory and some transnational feminist theories, particularly given his emphasis on diagnosing and overcoming structural domination and injustice. However, she also questions whether his emphasis on a foundational notion of justice is compatible with feminist concerns and whether his theory has the resources to deal with issues of adaptive preferences.

Our volume closes with two final pieces: Amy Allen's reply to Forst's critique of her work in the opening chapter and Forst's reply to his critics in this volume.

NOTES

1. Martin Jay, *The Dialectical Imagination: A History of the Frankfurt School and the Institute for Social Research, 1923–1950* (Boston: Little, Brown, 1973), 10.

2. Max Horkheimer, *Between Philosophy and Social Science: Selected Early Writings*, trans. G. Frederick Hunter, Matthew S. Kramer, and John Torpey (Cambridge, MA: MIT Press, 1993), 1–14.

3. Both of these essays can be found in Max Horkheimer, *Critical Theory: Selected Essays*, trans. J. O'Connell et al. (New York: Herder and Herder, 1972), 188–252.

4. Horkheimer, "Traditional and Critical Theory," in *Critical Theory*, 198–99. The German text reads, "Die Selbterkenntnis des Menschen in der Gegenwart ist jedoch nicht die mathematische Naturwissenschaft, die als ewiger Logos eschient, sondern die von Interesse an vernünftigen Zuständen durchherrschte kritische Theorie der bestehenden Gesellschaft"; Max Horkheimer, *Gesammelte Schriften, Band 4: Schriften 1936–1941* (Frankfurt am Main: Fischer Taschenbuch Verlag, 1988), 172.

5. Horkheimer, "Postscript," in *Critical Theory*, 246.

6. See Albrecht Wellmer, "On Critical Theory," *Social Research* 81, no. 3 (2014): 705–33, citation at 706.

7. Jürgen Habermas, *The Theory of Communicative Action*, trans. Thomas McCarthy, vol. 2, *Lifeworld and System: A Critique of Functionalist Reason* (Boston: Beacon, 1987), 378–79.

8. Ibid., 397.

9. Ibid., 402–3.

10. Ibid., 403.

11. Paul Ricoeur, *Freud & Philosophy: An Essay on Interpretation*, trans. Denis Savage (New Haven: Yale University Press, 1970), 33.

12. Ibid., 34.

13. Ibid.

14. Michèle Le Doeuff, *The Philosophical Imaginary*, trans. Colin Gordon (London: Continuum, 2002).

15. Willi Goetschel, *Constituting Critique: Kant's Writing as Critical Praxis*, trans. Eric Schwab (Durham: Duke University Press, 1994).

16. See Martin Jay, "Kant: Reason as Critique; the Critique of Reason," in *Reason After Its Eclipse: On Late Critical Theory*, 36–59 (Madison: University of Wisconsin Press, 2016).

17. Immanuel Kant, *Critique of Pure Reason*, trans. and ed. Paul Guyer and Allen Wood (Cambridge: Cambridge University Press, 1998), 100–101 (italics in the original). For the sake of comparison and completeness, here is Marcus Weigelt's Penguin translation:

> "It is clearly the result, not of carelessness but of the matured judgment of our age, which will no longer rest satisfied with the mere appearance of knowledge. It is, at the same time, a powerful appeal to reason to undertake anew the most difficult of tasks, namely that of self-knowledge, and to institute a court of appeal which should protect reason in its rightful claims, but dismiss all groundless pretensions, and to do this not by means of despotic decrees but according to the eternal and unalterable laws of reason. This court of appeal is no other than the *critique of pure reason* itself."

> Immanuel Kant, *Critique of Pure Reason*, trans. Marcus Weigelt (New York: Penguin, 2007), 7.

18. See Maria Chiara Pievatolo, "The Tribunal of Reason: Kant and Juridical Nature of Pure Reason," *Ratio Juris* 12, no. 3 (1999): 311–27.

19. Onora O'Neill, quoted in Jay, *Reason After Its Eclipse*, 53.

20. Jay, *Reason After Its Eclipse*, 55.

21. Here we recommend the important work of Drucilla Cornell, who has also been engaged in reclaiming Kant for the critical theory tradition. See her important *Moral Images of Freedom: A Future for Critical Theory* (Lanham, MD: Rowman & Littlefield, 2008), especially chap. 1: "Kantian Beginnings to the Legacy of Critical Theory: The Harmonious Play of Freedom."

22. Goetschel, *Constituting Critique*, 4–5.

23. Rainer Forst, *Contexts of Justice: Political Philosophy Beyond Liberalism and Communitarianism*, trans. John M. M. Farrell (Berkeley: University of California Press, 2002), 5.

24. Rainer Forst, *Toleration in Conflict: Past and Present*, trans. Ciaran Cronin (Cambridge: Cambridge University Press, 2012).

25. Ibid., 27.

26. Ibid., 28.

27. Ibid., 29.

28. Wendy Brown and Rainer Forst, *The Power of Tolerance: A Debate*, ed. Luca di Blasi and Christoph F. E. Holzhey (New York: Columbia University Press, 2014), 31 (italics added).

29. Rainer Forst, *Das Recht auf Rechtfertigung: Elemente einer konstruktivitischen Theorie der Gerechtkeit* (Frankfurt am Main: Suhrkamp Verlag, 2007).

30. Rainer Forst, *The Right to Justification: Elements of a Constructivist Theory of Justice*, trans. Jeffrey Flynn (New York: Columbia University Press, 2011).

31. Ibid., 4–5.

32. Rainer Forst, "The Concept of Progress," in *Normativity and Power: Analyzing Social Orders of Justification*, trans. Ciaran Cronin (New York: Oxford University Press, 2017), 69–74.

33. Ibid., 73.

34. Ibid.

35. Forst, "Noumenal Power," in *Normativity and Power*, 37–51.

36. Ibid., 38.

37. Ibid., 51.

38. See Amy Allen, *The End of Progress: Decolonizing the Normative Foundations of Critical Theory* (New York: Columbia University Press, 2016), chap. 4.

CHAPTER 2

The Justification of Progress and the Progress of Justification

Rainer Forst

1.

The concept of progress is dialectical in nature. On the one hand, progress is a necessary term for anyone who is interested in human emancipation understood as overcoming social domination (which I call "moral-political progress") or anyone interested in improving people's living conditions by medical means (which I call "progress in life conditions"), for example. On the other hand, some of those who are engaged in struggles for emancipation think that this implies overcoming the very concept of progress being, as Ashis Nandy[1] says, one of the "dirtiest" words, a word that all too often did and still does justify domination across and within societies. It seems to be wedded to a universalist teleological form of thinking according to which some societies or groups have reached that telos earlier than others and thus have the authority—and maybe even the mission—to pull the less progressed people out of their "self-incurred immaturity" into the light of reason and freedom, possibly even overcoming their ignorant or indolent reluctance by force. As Amy Allen emphasizes, the idea of progress is deeply entangled with imperialist universalisms of this kind, "nourished by a philosophical and cultural imaginary that justifies the political subjugation of distant territories and their native populations through claims that such peoples are less advanced, cognitively inferior, and therefore naturally subordinate."[2] This critique points to the essential aspect of the dialectic implicit in the concept of progress—namely, the tension between its normative and its historical meaning, between the ideal expressed and the reality it stands for. Could it be, as some argue, that the reality of domination weighs so heavily that no ideal content can be saved for that term such that dialectics come to an end? Or can we, as I believe, and furthermore, should we develop a dereified, nonteleological, nondominating, emancipatory conception of progress? Otherwise, what shall we call social developments through which relations of colonial (or neocolonial) domination are overcome through social struggle? If we can't avoid calling such developments social progress, we must carefully reflect on those standards for progress that do not lead to new forms of domination under the guise of liberation, possibly hidden from sight. Nevertheless, such standards must exist if we do not want to give up the language of progress altogether.

I believe that we are unavoidably caught in the dialectic of progress: If our critique of false notions of progress is *situated* and not merely abstract and empty, we also argue *for* progress, both in theory and in practice, because overcoming false progress is true progress. Being against progress because one is motivated by an account of nondomination or emancipation is also to be for it, and I don't see how we, who understand ourselves as participants and not merely distant observers of history, could (as Allen suggests) say that we should not be committed to any backward-looking claim to progress and yet still hold on to a contextual, forward-looking imperative of progress.[3] That strikes me as a contradictory and ahistorical view that refuses to learn from history, a history containing regress as well as (we hope) progress, whatever criteria of emancipation we use. Especially in our role as critical theorists, the critique of domination in its many forms—economic, racial, or sexist (or a combination thereof)—obliges us to think of ourselves as participants in ongoing struggles for emancipation (whether successful or not), struggles that did not begin with us.

2.

A proper understanding of the contemporary discussion about the concept of progress requires us to make a distinction between two major fields of discourse already alluded to.[4] On the one hand, in many societies, there is a debate over the appropriate definition of technological progress as qualitative progress in life conditions: How much environmental destruction does unfettered economic growth bring with it? What is our stance on artificially modifying food or on genetically improving human nature? What is permitted in medical research? These are genuine evaluative questions concerning progress in specific areas of science, technology, and economics that examine its social costs. In pluralistic societies, it is not unusual that such debates involve clashes between very different value systems such that the search for shared norms proves to be difficult.

19

On the other hand, there are debates about progress that also call for a normative language, although one of a different kind. In such cases, resistance to certain conceptions of progress is fueled less by ethical evaluations of a desirable way of life than by an impulse of justice—one that demands what I call "moral-political progress." What is deplored are social or economic structures that are dominating—that is, lack sufficient justification among those who are subjected to them—and what is revealed is a desire for emancipation that should not be confused with a general form of skepticism concerning progress. The targets of such criticism are unjustifiable and imposed conceptions of development that "colonize" social lifeworlds, to use Habermas's expression—also in an effort to "develop," "modernize," and sometimes even to "liberate" societies.[5] Whether it is powerful states, associations of states, or international organizations (in cooperation with certain groups within a society) that are accused of neocolonialism does not change the fact that here it is essentially a matter of how social and political power is structured and organized—and of how much social self-determination is possible in a globalized society. These conflicts are not simply a matter of being for or against "globalization," however, because many of the global political and economic relations that are criticized as asymmetrical cannot be changed except through global coordination.[6] Such criticism is not just directed against external domination, since it most often also criticizes internal domination—that is, a lack of justification and of justificatory standing within a given normative order.[7]

20 Both debates—but especially the latter—show that the discussions about the concept of progress should not be viewed in terms of a simple pro or contra. Instead, we must keep the social dimension of these controversies in mind. Then the question is often not whether a society should "develop" but who determines this process and defines the corresponding goals. The decisive question raised by the concept of moral-political progress remains how the power to define such progress and the paths leading to it is structured.

3.

With this we arrive at an important insight. Although the concept of progress is used in a normative sense in the two fields of debate mentioned, it is not a normative concept in its own right. Technological progress cannot count as social progress in life conditions without social evaluations of what it is good for, who benefits from it, and what costs it generates. Nor can true social progress as moral-political progress exist where the changes in question are enforced and experienced as colonization. Technological progress must be socially accepted, and socially accepted progress is progress that is determined and brought about by the members of the society in question. Democratic political forms and procedures therefore are primarily seen not as development *goals* but as essential *conditions* of social advancement such that the goal of democracy ought not to be attained by nondemocratic means—and that progress in life conditions achieved, say, by a technocratic, authoritarian regime cannot counterbalance the lack of moral-political progress in political and social justice. Of particular importance in this regard are the many "empowerment" initiatives, such as political initiatives in civil-society forums and organizations or economic empowerment measures—for example, through microcredits or more comprehensive social policy measures, especially those where underprivileged groups (in many countries, first and foremost, women) win participation rights through social struggles. Increasing the scope of agency for individuals and collectives, as Amartya Sen emphasizes, is the central means and goal of development and progress.[8]

As the example of contemporary China demonstrates, in an age of multiple modernities, there is no universally valid script for the combination of economic, cultural, and political modernization in the sense of democratization. But in the long run, it is doubtful whether the one can succeed without the other. A regime is strengthened by increases in prosperity, but it is simultaneously tested and placed in question by technical capabilities and by new upwardly mobile social groups. Social dynamics lead to political dynamics. However, such processes do not unfold along a single, predictable path. This may be unsettling for those who hope to derive prognostic wisdom from sociological research about modernization, yet, normatively speaking, that is also a good thing because every process that deserves to be called progress should be one that those subjected to it initiate and control themselves. This is difficult enough. But once again, it becomes apparent that the evaluative criteria for progress refer to the concept of nondomination and self-determination—as a fundamental requirement of justice understood as an autonomous and collective *practice,* not as a teleologically fixed result.

This seems to give rise to a dilemma. I began by emphasizing the critique of unilateral Western notions of social development and progress, but now a series of normative concepts, such as autonomy, democracy, and justice, which seem to owe their existence to a Western political and cultural background, come back into play. Have we reverted from criticizing a form of particularism that disguises itself as universalism back to this very particularism? With this fear we must contrast a different perspective, for the critique of the unilateral or imposed, of the dominating and oppressive idea of progress or of the corresponding practice, is, to repeat, itself normative, and it calls for nothing less than collectively self-determined forms of social development. This language therefore is the authentic language of progress, and what critics as well as proponents of the idea of progress must recognize is that progress is a *reflexive* concept: every progressive process must be constantly questioned as to whether it is in the social interest of those who are part of this process.

4.

The true logic of progress is not primarily a social-technical, scientific, or technological logic of reaching a certain telos; rather, it is a social logic in the sense that it must be supported and defined by the members of a normative order themselves. There are no predetermined blueprints for this, though there is a reflexive principle of justice as justification, which states that only those who are subjected to such an order may define the steps that constitute its "progress." This is in line with the basic principle of discursive justice as nondomination, which states that no one may be subjected to specific rules or institutions that cannot be adequately justified to him or her as a free and equal normative authority. That is the core meaning of self-determination that is central to social progress. It implies a basic human "right to justification," which is as much a right to the protection of individuals as a right to equal participation in social and political decision-making processes.[9] According to this principle, progress means that a society successfully strives for new levels of justification that ensure not only that political and social relations can be justified in a reciprocal and general way but also that there are institutions for producing such justifications in autonomous discursive practices in the first place.[10] Hence the justification of progress can only be achieved if those who are subjected to the social order that changes are themselves the agents determining this change through processes of justification—and real progress consists in setting up frameworks for justification that overcome domination in the sense of persons or groups not being respected as free and equal authorities of justification. The justification of progress lies in the progress of justification as a social practice among equals.

I want to argue that the concept of justification is crucial to understanding and evaluating social progress. But we need to conceive of social progress in the right way and avoid reified and dominating ways of thinking about what a structure of justification is or what it means to be respected as a justificatory equal. In short, we must understand progress in nonteleological terms and conceive of it in a *deontological,* process-oriented way: the imperative for progress is, as Allen also says, the imperative of emancipation as "the minimization of domination"[11]—or as I would add, that of overcoming domination. There is no fixed ideal or telos that would predetermine what this means, as the participants *themselves* will be the sole agents who justify this in discursive practice, taking their guidance from the criteria of reciprocity and generality. Any theory that calls itself critical needs to stress this, for, to adopt Bernard Williams's rendering of the basic Habermasian insight of discursive nondomination, "the acceptance of a justification does not count if the acceptance itself is produced by the coercive power which is supposedly being justified."[12] This is why true liberation and progress consists in the autonomous creation of conditions of nondomination and mutual justification.

23

The imperative of progress Allen wants to hold on to is an imperative of "genuine respect and openness to the Other,"[13] taking the agency of others seriously, avoiding any conception of others as "not yet capable of autonomous self-rule,"[14] and in addition realizing the central value of freedom.[15] I agree with all of this. But I fail to see how the thoroughly Rortyan "metanormative contextualism"[16] that Allen advocates could serve that purpose. How can standards for evaluating progress in a postcolonial age be reparticularized and reparochialized in the way she suggests—that is, by appealing to "the normative inheritance of modernity, particularly to its notions of freedom, inclusion and equal respect"?[17] Was it not precisely *that* inheritance, according to Allen herself, that dominated the allegedly unfree and unreasonable "others"? Of course, she uses this contextualism to remind the moderns of their contingent heritage and to respect other cultures with "humility"[18] about their own standpoint. But that has major disadvantages because it still implies that the West or, even worse, modernity is the true normative source of universal freedom, equality, and respect and that other cultures are not really participating in this history, or if they are, they do so primarily as victims of the oppressive implications of these values historically understood. So it is "we" (Westerners) who have to do better this time. But again the "others" (non-Westerners)—occasionally referred to as the "subaltern," using Gayatri Spivak's term (albeit in a much less dialectical way than Spivak herself)[19]—seem to be outside of this normative horizon, only this time, "we" ought to treat them as dialogue partners rather than as objects of domination. But we only do so because "we" are moderns and they are not. So it seems, according to Allen, that we do not share any normative framework with them—that is, we still *impose* ours, but this time in a friendly, humble, nonoppressive way.

So what exactly is the normative standing of these "others"—who are they? Implicitly, I think, Allen's answer is clear: they are our justificatory equals, and we must not impose our normative order on them. Explicitly, however, she says the opposite: we do not share a normative status with them, since we do not share any normative basis according to Allen's relativistic framework; thus we regard these "others" as alien but treat them with respect because we as moderns think that this is the right thing to do. But that is a unilateral, generous move on our part, the metanormative contextualist says. We ought to be open to learn from them about what they think, but there is no common moral language binding us all—for such a language of, say, them having a right to justification would impose an alien and dominating framework upon them. According to Allen, it is to force a notion of reason on "others" that disempowers them and leaves them speechless and justificationless and that presumes a universalism that does not exist. According to Allen, any framework of Kantian-style practical reason "explicitly or implicitly excludes, represses, or dominates all that is associated with the so-called *Other of reason,* whether that be understood in terms of madness, irrationality, the emotions, the affects, embodiment, or the imagination, all of which are symbolically associated with black, queer, female, colonized, and subaltern subjects."[20]

But I believe that the opposite is the case. I think that the right to justification accords the "subaltern" precisely the voice that they can claim as justificatory equals, including the voice that criticizes dominant discourses of justification. In virtue of its reflexive and critical character, the right to justification is the right to question any reification of justification and the noumenal power structures that deny a voice to certain groups who are deemed "unreasonable."[21] So to deny others such standing as justificatory equals in the name of particularism about justification is the wrong way to go; it just reproduces the dominating image of "us" as moderns and of others as nonmodern, nonreasonable "others" who are completely different from us—a form of alienating others that I call *reverse orientalism*. This critique is in line with Edward Said's powerful reflections on orientalism, a particular form of "othering" in an imperialist, racist, and ethnocentric mode, denying these others a voice and a sense of justice.[22] In a powerful afterword from 1995, Said criticizes romanticizing and essentializing readings of his critique that celebrate the "other" and combine postmodern and postcolonial thought in the wrong way by no longer criticizing the perversions of the "grand narratives of emancipation and enlightenment" but giving up the general imperative of emancipation.[23] With Said, I want to uphold this imperative, and with him I want to affirm that "the subaltern *can* speak, as the history of liberation movements in the twentieth century eloquently attests."[24]

To be sure, Allen thoroughly reflects on this issue, since it goes to the heart of her enterprise. As moderns, on a first level of normativity, we are, according to her, committed to modern values such as freedom and equality, but on a reflexive second level, we know that these commitments are parochial, contextual, and historical, and thus we will not impose them. They are not context-transcendent.[25] But here we need to ask, What does the metanormative level ask us to do? If it requires us to treat others with equal respect and engage in an "open-ended dialogue"[26] with them, as Allen wants us to do, what is the metanormative framework for that kind of discursive respect? It is the right to justification, expressing a context-transcending imperative—what else could it be? To deny this and still hold on to the imperative of equal respect is flatly contradictory.

Otherwise, to repeat, we leave the others in a normative void. Whereas some might generously interpret "the normative horizon of Enlightenment modernity" as taking "openness to criticism and reflexivity as normative goals," being "willing to unlearn,"[27] others are simply happy parochialists—that is, neocolonial, imperialist modern fascists who want to make an empire great again and interpret Enlightenment modernity as licensing that. What do we say to them—that they got modernity wrong? But we just learned from Allen that modernity harbors a lot of imperialist racism and fascism. So modernistic contextualism is a no-go unless it is countered by the universalism of justificatory equality, according to which each person has a justified claim to the same status of being a normative authority. In short, if false universalism based on parochialism is the problem, enlightened particularism is not the solution. The only solution is enlightened, self-critical universalism, since it is the only one that equips the excluded with a right to justification and critique.

We—as critics arguing and fighting for emancipation—express our *no* to the dominating parochialists, whether they argue in a particularist ("this is how we live around here") or false universalist way ("we live the true way of life" or "we belong to the master race"), and we take our stance against racism, sexism, economic exploitation, and cultural and social humiliation to be as foundational as it can be—as did and do those who argued against slavery, torture, or political or sexual oppression. Such foundationalism is not a stance of authoritarianism, as Allen claims in her critique of my approach,[28] but exactly the opposite because it emphasizes the necessary authority to *resist* authoritarianism, whether contextualist or universalist. If you want to resist oppression, your stance better be as strong as it can be. And if you resist fascism, you do not "invite" the fascist to see things your way in a nonfoundationalist exchange; rather, you are convinced that he is wrong and that is how you act and why you act. In other words, we do not have the liberty in this world to be the contextualists Allen wants us to be. We have to take a stance, and for that we need the authority to say *no* to domination. The *no* to false foundations is foundational.

People in other societies have the same right, and parochial contextualism does not serve these critics well either. We disenfranchise them from their own societies by looking at them through the lens of reverse orientalism, as if freedom and modernity were Western, modern values that we can use but they cannot. In my view—and this is where Allen and I are truly at odds—contextualism speaks the voice of the powerful because it relativizes the oppositional claim, silences critics, and tells them that they are out of tune with their society. Contextualism is the theory of the dominant who claim the interpretive privilege to define their culture and society and deny others their right to justification. But the *no* to racism, sexism, or other forms of domination is never nonfoundationalist, and it is never misplaced in *any* cultural context; it is just the voice of radical critique. The subaltern speak even where they are not heard, and they have the *right* to a voice wherever they are dominated and turned into the "subaltern" in an essentialist and dominating way.[29]

As Uma Narayan forcefully argues with respect to the rejection of gender as well as cultural essentialism, one needs to avoid both forms of identity and norm imposition:

> Postcolonial feminists have good reason to oppose many of the legacies of colonialism, as well as ongoing forms of economic exploitation and political domination by Western nations at the international level. However, I do not think that such an agenda is well served either by uncritically denigrating values and practices that appear to be in some sense "Western" or by indiscriminately valorizing values and practices that appear "Non-Western." Political rhetoric that polarizes "Western" and "Non-Western" values risks obscuring the degree to which economic and political agendas, carried out in collaboration between particular Western and Third World elites, work to erode the rights and quality of life for many citizens in both Western and Third World contexts.[30]

Narayan not only points to the reality of multiple domination that needs to be captured in ways that avoid one-sided social analyses; she also shows why false universalism that imposes a notion of "sameness" on others and thus leads to the imposition of Western normative orders on other societies in order to dominate them has to be rejected. The same applies to false notions of "difference" that essentialize and unify other societies and thus silence critical voices within them, as if to call for respect for women's rights were an "alien" and alienating claim in a non-Western society, "leaving feminists susceptible to attacks as 'Westernized cultural traitors' who suffer from a lack of appreciation for 'their traditions' and respect for 'their culture.'"[31] This is a form of what Michel Foucault once called "enlightenment blackmail,"[32] which we should resist regardless of whether it comes from a reified form of Enlightenment thought or from a reified form of anti-Enlightenment thought. We need to recognize (with Said and Narayan) that it can equally be an orientalist, postcolonial form of blackmail: either to be uncritically for "enlightened" forms of modern political and social life while ignoring their dominating aspects or to be against them and thus ignore the dominating effects of "authentic" non-Western forms of life, celebrating them as the "other" of modernity, thus essentializing them.

5.

I think that the *no* to domination, insofar as it appeals to the right to justification, is the voice of subaltern reason, since reason is the critical faculty of justification and·domination is the denial of justification and of justificatory standing to persons, restricting the justification community in an arbitrary way when it comes to matters of moral concern, as Richard Rorty did, for example, by questioning the idea of a universal moral language.[33] Yet since morality is a set of universal norms that claim to be reciprocally and generally justifiable, restricting morality to a justification community in an arbitrary, culturally biased way is unjustifiable and irrational. This is why we cannot be radical contextualists about reason when it comes to epistemic and moral truth claims. Rejecting radical contextualism means that we can, of course, be wrong in thinking that we found the best justification for a claim to truth, but it also implies that there are general criteria for such a debate.[34] To criticize reified notions of rationality for excluding some as "other"—as mad, for example—of course implies that these others are rational, according to a nonreified notion of reason, not that they are really an "other" of reason.

A theory cannot claim to be "critical" unless it seeks explicit reassurance about its concept of reason and subjects it to criticism,[35] for no matter how much critical theory opposes the "pathologies of reason" in modernity, nevertheless, as Axel Honneth emphasizes, it always subjects "universality—which should, at the same time, be both embodied by and realized through social cooperation—to the standards of rational justification."[36] Hence I conclude (pace Honneth) that no other concepts—for example, concepts of the "good"—can take the place of the imperative and the criteria of rational justification. A historical a priori claiming priority over the imperative of reciprocal and general justification, such that it could determine what counts as genuine progress and what does not, is therefore impossible. The kind of "normative reconstruction" of the "promise of freedom"[37] of modern societies undertaken by Honneth presupposes that the "moral rationality"[38] that is supposed to become effective in realizing individual freedom points beyond the established institutions. But then the reflexive and justificatory pressure exerted by individuals and groups on social institutions is not bound to a "pre-given" ethical life or promise, and the critique of injustice is not only able to look, as Honneth claims following Georg Hegel, "just beyond the horizon of existing ethical life."[39] On the contrary, it can see as far as reciprocal-general justification permits or demands. To paraphrase Heidegger, the normative possibility of freedom has a higher status than its normative reality.[40]

The only form of progressive critique that merits the name is one oriented to rational standards of justifiability in a socially situated way. That critique is always "immanent" in the sense that it takes the status quo as its starting point as trivial; what is not obvious, however, is the demand that it should orient itself to "settled," "pre-given," "accepted," or "inherent" norms.[41] There are forms of criticism of which this is true because they reveal the explicit or implicit contradictions within an order of justification in an immanent way—and with good reasons. But that the reasons in question are good does *not* follow from the fact that one appeals to accepted or inherent norms. Libertarians who criticize capitalism for not adhering consistently enough to the market principle and thus becoming mired in contradictions also argue in an immanent way that appeals to systemic features of capitalism. But they cannot justify their criticism toward those who, qua free and equal persons, should be the authorities who determine which economic system can be politically justified, insofar as market processes undermine this very authority (as must be shown in a justice-based analysis).[42] Hence the fact that a critique is immanent is neither a reason for nor a hallmark of its legitimacy. A radical critique that rejects an entire historically developed understanding of the market, by contrast, may have much more going for it. And a critique that seeks to transform a liberal understanding of the market into a socialist one will hardly be able to justify this in a purely "immanent" way—nor will it have to. Radical criticism may be immanent *or* transcending such that it is no longer clear where the one form of criticism ends and the other begins—as, for example, when Luther described the pope as the true "Antichrist," the Levellers declared the king to be the servant of the people "by the grace of God," or Marx saw bourgeois society as a context of modern slavery. Settled ethical life is the *object* of criticism, not its *ground* or *limit*. To recall the words of Theodor Adorno, "The limit of immanent critique is that the law of the immanent context is ultimately one with the delusion that has to be overcome."[43]

These remarks bear on a further problem—namely, that of the *historicity* of the normative foundations of progressive criticism. Should we consider the criteria of reason or normativity as "historically contingent," as Seyla Benhabib, for example, argues when she describes the right to justification as "a contingent legacy of struggles against slavery, oppression, inequality, degradation, and humiliation over centuries" and accordingly as a historic "achievement"?[44] As I tried to show in my historical analysis of the development of the practice of toleration in its many different forms and justifications, we do in fact have to understand such concepts against the background of concrete historical processes of which we ourselves are part. This enables us to see how the demand for reciprocal and general justifications gave rise and continues to give rise to a historical dynamic that forces existing conceptions and justifications to go beyond themselves—always in a dialectical process, involving new attempts to bring this dynamic to a close.[45] If we want to distinguish in a historically situated, dialectical way between emancipatory and nonemancipatory struggles and developments and to view certain developments as "achievements" or "learning processes," we cannot assume that our assessment of them is merely "contingent"— that is, the arbitrary product of these developments. Think of Williams's critical-theory principle mentioned earlier—an evaluation produced by what is evaluated is not sufficiently justified. This rules out historicism about the standards of critique.

Of course, we cannot claim that certain developments are "necessary" either, for want of an equivalent to Hegel's absolute. Finite reason does not have access to a "worldless" standpoint from which it can regard its own norms from a distance as "merely contingent" or to a divine standpoint of the *Weltgeist* from which it could recognize historical necessity. From a finite rational perspective that understands itself as practical, the principle of justification is *the* principle of reason and the right to justification is its moral implication—no more but no less either. There is no transcendent perspective from which its contingency *or* necessity could be ascertained, but we have no need of such a perspective either. The only perspective to which we have access is that of a participant, not one of a transhistorical observer.

Consistency demands that we recognize that the pioneers of emancipation developed their positions in societies in which they were regarded as immoral or crazy by the dominant standards of justification—for example, the aforementioned radical Levellers or Pierre Bayle, who defended the thesis, which was frowned upon at the time, that even atheists are capable of being moral—and that reason is a faculty of justification independent of religion.[46] Should we follow the historicist in saying that what first made these positions true was that they won out over time and hence that they were *not justified* when these radical thinkers were alive? Should we join with those who condemned Bayle and others in crying "heresy" because this corresponded to the order of justification valid at the time? Could we ever understand and valorize emancipatory and radical criticism on this basis—the criticism of those who in their own day spoke a language in which they called slavery a crime and not a form of benevolence, in which they called tyranny by its name and not a divine right, and in which intolerance no longer counted as service to God but instead as brutal violence? If we view these languages as "achievements," then we can regard them not as either contingent or necessary but only as *moral progress,* as progress in our moral self-understanding through *morally justified* innovation but not through historical "success." The latter would represent a form of moral Darwinism in which the winners decide what constitutes moral truth. But this would have nothing to do with critical theory. "Prevailing" historically cannot define the criteria for what counts as success in evaluative terms; only critical reason can.

But reason does not elevate itself to a superhistorical power in this regard either. It is only convinced here and now of what counted and

31

counts as reasonable. The twofold analysis of orders of justification as historically occurring social facts and as orders with a claim to justification that opens them up to criticism enables us to say that, even though certain criticisms were considered to be unjustified in their time, they were nevertheless justified from a superior normative point of view because they brought the principle of justification itself to bear—even if, as is most often the case, they did not win out in history.[47]

The perspective outlined enables us to define a conception of *progress* that cannot be suspected of disguising ethnocentrisms. Only those processes can count as moral-political progress that break open orders of justification in ways that make new forms of reciprocal and general justification possible so that those affected can determine *themselves* in which direction their society should develop. In this way, the notion of progress can be prevented from becoming an instrument through which social and political autonomy is lost—for example, by other economically or politically powerful societies or institutions dictating to a society how it should develop. Genuine progress occurs where new levels of justification are made accessible or are achieved through struggles that turn subjects into justificatory authorities in the first place. Comprehensive progress involves more than just the existence of better-justified social relations (e.g., ones involving a higher standard of living). It occurs when the justification conditions within a society are such that a basic structure of justification begins to develop. Discursive autonomy is realized only in internal processes and procedures, not in conditions imposed from the outside. A critical theory cannot dispense with such a concept of progress.

6.

In his treatise on *African Philosophy Through Ubuntu*, Mogobe Ramose, one of the great African philosophers, defends the "African's inalienable right to reason" as a means toward "the authentic liberation of Africa."[48] This right to reason independently from the concepts and noumenal powers of the colonizers, past and present, means, on the one hand, criticizing the "will to dominate," which "currently manifests itself in the name of 'democratization,' 'globalization' and 'human rights.'"[49] On the other hand, it means developing a critical reconsideration of what democracy, globalization, and human rights mean from an African perspective. On the basis of an ontology of belonging together historically and morally called "Ubuntu," Ramose claims that the search for an emancipatory politics is a search for democracy based on African traditions of consensus seeking, not following Western models of party rivalry, for example.[50] And with respect to economic globalization, Ramose argues that we need to overcome a global system of exploitation that "translates the questionable metaphysics of the dogma of thou shalt kill in pursuit of individual survival into practice"[51] and should start to take human rights for Africans, such as the right to life, seriously. I wholeheartedly agree with Allen that we need to enter into a dialogue with thinkers like Ramose and many others—but what we learn from them is not just something about cultural difference; rather, we learn something about the real problems of our world, the brutalities of the various forms of domination that exist, including, not least, economic domination. That is what critical theory is about, and that is what we learn from a dialogue with others who are not simply "others" in a global world. For critical theory, the main problem is not reason but the destruction of reason (to use György Lukács's term) that goes on in many parts of the world in a systematic way.

33

Otherwise, if we cut ourselves off from the struggles of others and ontologize cultural differences, we will not be able to do what Spivak asks us to do—namely, to develop a "transnational literacy"[52] that allows us to criticize transnational forms of domination and to engage in transnational struggles for justice. Such a conception of justice cannot be imposed on multiple social contexts but must be developed discursively—but for that to happen, a common normative framework of moral equality and claims to discursive autonomy must exist. If such a framework is missing, any transnational moral-political language, including a critical one, is an imposition.

In a similar spirit, Achille Mbembe argues for a critical theory that provides the social-analytic tools to identify "transnational networks of repression" that combine "foreign corporations, powerful nations, and local dominant classes"[53] into what I call situations of "multiple domination." In my view, a critical theory of transnational justice must start from such forms of domination.[54] This includes analyzing the power structures of religious, economic, and political domination that deny the development of an autonomous form of political thinking in African societies, as Mbembe points out.[55] The first task is to reclaim what I call noumenal power, which Mbembe links to life itself: "To have power is therefore to know how to give and to receive forms. But it is also to know how to escape existing forms, how to change everything while remaining the same, to marry new forms of life and constantly enter into new relationships with destruction, loss, and death."[56] The struggle against destructive and for autonomous creative power is of both a local and a transnational nature: "Whatever the location, epoch, or context in which they take place, the horizon of such struggles remains the same: how to belong fully in this world that is common to all of us, how to pass from the status of the excluded to the status of the right-holder, how to participate in the construction and the distribution of the world. . . . The path is clear: on the basis of a critique of the past, we must create a future that is inseparable from the notions of justice, dignity, and the in-common."[57]

If the language of human rights, self-determination, and transnational justice—properly defined and reappropriated—is the language of progress, as Ramose and Mbembe argue, then this is not primarily a historical or a sociological insight or demand. Rather, it follows as a moral imperative from the critique of false ideas of progress as well as from the critique of the prevention of social progress, for emancipation from a situation of oppression and exploitation is a human right, now and at all times. We are therefore bound to adhere to this concept of progress as long as forms of human domination exist and as long as there is a moral imperative to overcome them. The struggle for emancipation requires a universal moral language that relativism betrays.

NOTES

I am indebted to the participants of the conference "Justification and Emancipation" at Penn State University in April 2017 for a discussion of the paper that became this chapter and from which I have greatly benefitted—with special thanks to Amy Allen and Eduardo Mendieta for making this event possible. I am also grateful to the participants in the conference "Normative Orders in Transition" at Goethe University Frankfurt in June 2017, where I presented this paper, and to Lea Ypi for her written comments on an earlier version. My thanks also to Paul Kindermann and Ciaran Cronin for their help in preparing this text.

35

1. Ashis Nandy, "Fortschritt," in *Vielfalt der Moderne—Ansichten der Moderne*, ed. Hans Joas (Frankfurt am Main: Fischer, 2012), 53.

2. Amy Allen, *The End of Progress: Decolonizing the Normative Foundations of Critical Theory* (New York: Columbia University Press, 2016), 2.

3. Ibid., 127.

4. The following section is adapted from my essay "The Concept of Progress," in Forst, *Normativity and Power: Analyzing Social Orders of Justification,* trans. Ciaran Cronin (Oxford: Oxford University Press, 2017), chap. 4.

5. See James Tully, "On Law, Democracy and Imperialism," in *Public Philosophy in a New Key,* ed. James Tully, vol. 2, *Imperialism and Civic Freedom* (Cambridge: Cambridge University Press, 2008), 127–65. See also Dorothea Gädeke, *Politik der Beherrschung: Eine kritische Theorie externer Demokratieförderung* (Berlin: Suhrkamp, 2017).

6. See Tom Hale, David Held, and Kevin Young, *Gridlock: Why Global Cooperation Is Failing Us When We Need It Most* (Cambridge: Polity, 2013).

7. For an evolutionary theory of moral progress that focuses on the question of equal status, see Allen Buchanan and Russell Powell, *The Evolution of Moral Progress: A Biocultural Theory* (Oxford: Oxford University Press, 2018).

8. Amartya Sen, *Development as Freedom* (Oxford: Oxford University Press, 2001).

9. See Rainer Forst, *The Right to Justification: Elements of a Constructivist Theory of Justice,* trans. Jeffrey Flynn (New York: Columbia University Press, 2012); Rainer Forst, *Justification and Critique: Towards a Critical Theory of Politics,* trans. Ciaran Cronin (Cambridge: Polity, 2014).

10. I trace such a logic of progress with reference to the question of toleration in Rainer Forst, *Toleration in Conflict: Past and Present,* trans. Ciaran Cronin (Cambridge: Cambridge University Press, 2013).

11. Allen, *End of Progress,* xiv.

12. Bernard Williams, *In the Beginning Was the Deed: Realism and Moralism in Political Argument* (Princeton: Princeton University Press, 2008), 6.

13. Allen, *End of Progress,* 33.

14. Ibid., 155.

15. Ibid., 195.

16. Ibid., 121.

17. Ibid., 33.

18. Ibid., 75.

19. Ibid., 152. For Spivak's dialectical critique of Kant, see Gayatri Chakravorty Spivak, *A Critique of Postcolonial Reason: Toward a History of the Vanishing Present* (Cambridge: Harvard University Press, 2000), chap. 1. For an interpretation, see Franziska Dübgen, *Was ist gerecht? Kennzeichen einer transnationalen solidarischen Politik* (Frankfurt am Main: Campus Verlag, 2014).

20. Allen, *End of Progress,* 137.

21. If, for example, the subaltern "define themselves as subjects on patriarchal terms or they allow themselves to be constituted as objects of imperialism" (ibid., 153), they are subjected to exactly the kinds of noumenal power structures this concept is meant to capture. See my *Normativity and Power*, chap. 2.

22. See Edward Said, *Orientalism* (London: Penguin, 2003), 201 and 281.

23. Ibid., 329–52.

24. Ibid., 335.

25. Allen, *End of Progress*, 211.

26. Ibid., 210.

27. Ibid., 218.

28. Ibid., 221.

29. See Dübgen, *Was ist gerecht?* See also Mattias Iser, *Empörung und Fortschritt: Grundlagen einer kritischen Theorie der Gesellschaft* (Frankfurt am Main: Campus Verlag, 2008).

30. Uma Narayan, "Essence of Culture and a Sense of History: A Feminist Critique of Cultural Essentialism," *Hypatia* 13, no. 2 (1998): 99.

31. Ibid., 102.

32. Michel Foucault, "What Is Enlightenment?," in *The Foucault Reader*, ed. Paul Rabinow (London: Penguin, 1984), 42.

33. Richard Rorty, *Contingency, Irony and Solidarity* (Cambridge: Cambridge University Press, 1989).

34. In the following, I use arguments from my introduction to *Normativity and Power*.

35. On this, see in general Jürgen Habermas, *The Theory of Communicative Action*, trans. Thomas McCarthy, 2 vols. (Boston: Beacon, 1984, 1987).

36. Axel Honneth, *Pathologies of Reason: On the Legacy of Critical Theory*, trans. James Ingram (New York: Columbia University Press, 2009), 28.

37. Axel Honneth, *Freedom's Right: The Social Foundations of Democratic Life*, trans. Joseph Ganahl (New York: Columbia University Press, 2014), viii.

38. Ibid., 2.

39. Ibid., 8 (in German: "knapp über den Horizont der existierenden Sittlichkeit").

40. Martin Heidegger, *Sein und Zeit*, 19th ed. (Tübingen: Max Niemeyer Verlag, 2006), 38: "Höher als die Wirklichkeit steht die *Möglichkeit*."

41. The two latter provisions can be found in Rahel Jaeggi, *Kritik von Lebensformen* (Berlin: Suhrkamp, 2014), 297 and 288.

42. See Forst, *Right to Justification*, chap. 8.

43. Theodor Adorno, *Negative Dialectics*, trans. E. B. Ashton (New York: Continuum, 1973), 182.

44. Seyla Benhabib, "The Uses and Abuses of Kantian Rigorism: On Rainer Forst's Moral and Political Philosophy," *Political Theory* 43, no. 6 (2015): 777–92, here 784. In what follows, I draw on my reply in "The Right to Justification: Moral and Political, Transcendental and Historical," 822–37. These questions concerning justification are also the focus of my discussion with Stephen White, "Does Critical Theory Need Strong Foundations?," *Philosophy & Social Criticism* 41, no. 3 (2015): 207–11; and my reply, "A Critical Theory of Politics: Grounds, Method and Aims," 225–34. See also Amy Allen, "The Power of Justification," in *Justice, Democracy and the Right to Justification*, ed. Rainer Forst (London: Bloomsbury, 2014), 65–86; Andrea Sangiovanni, "Scottish Constructivism and the Right to Justification,"

in *Justice, Democracy and the Right to Justification*, 29–64; Anthony Laden, "The Practice of Equality," in *Justice, Democracy and the Right to Justification*, 103–26; and my reply "Justifying Justification: Reply to my Critics," in *Justice, Democracy and the Right to Justification*, 169–216.

45. See Forst, *Toleration in Conflict*.

46. On this, see my "Religion and Toleration from the Enlightenment to the Post-secular Era: Bayle, Kant and Habermas," in *Normativity and Power*, chap. 5.

47. On this, see my interpretation of Bayle in "Religion and Toleration."

48. Mogobe Ramose, *African Philosophy Through Ubuntu*, trans. Laurent Dubois (Harare: Mond Books, 2005), 4.

49. Ibid., 6.

50. Ibid., 101.

51. Ibid., 147.

52. Spivak, *Critique of Postcolonial Reason*, 399.

53. Achille Mbembe, *Critique of Black Reason* (Durham: Duke University Press, 2017), 5.

54. See Forst, *Right to Justification*, 257.

55. Mbembe, *Critique of Black Reason*, 87–88.

56. Ibid., 132.

57. Ibid., 176–77.

CHAPTER 3

Autonomy and Justification

What Reasons Do We Owe Each Other and Ourselves?

John Christman

According to Rainer Forst, all members of a just society share a right to justification of the fundamental norms that govern them interpersonally and institutionally. A complement to this basic normative commitment is the respect for autonomy that all are owed, as expressed by this right to justification. Autonomy understood as self-government implies that agents can justify their own commitments to themselves—or at least accept them without alienation. This means that self-government has both an *inter*personal and an *intra*personal dimension: the way that we govern ourselves is that we are subject to reasons we can affirm for ourselves, and we govern each other collectively by giving and responding to reasons we all can affirm—or at least not reasonably reject. Theorists have had much to say about the dynamic of mutual justification among citizens through various mechanisms of democratic deliberation and public reason. Theorized in other contexts is also the internal dynamic of self-justification constitutive of autonomy that goes along with this dynamic. But little is said about the interaction between the two.

In this chapter, I want to explore this complementary dynamic as well as how these two lines of evaluation—of oneself and of others—interact. A crucial question that arises from this picture is whether the standards of *self*-justification (securing individual autonomy) are the same as the standards for interpersonal justification (for moral and political norms). I will proceed by discussing the interpersonal dynamics of moral and political justification, followed by an explication of the idea of personal autonomy (at least in a vein I favor). I then conclude with a discussion of their mutually implicating demands. Of special interest, however, will be whether these demands can be met or can continue to guide our critical social reflections and activities, when we take as seriously as we must the deep scars of injury and injustice that mark all our social geographies.

1. INTERPERSONAL JUSTIFICATION

In Forst's view, "Every moral norm must rest on a justification that corresponds to the criteria of reciprocity and generality. This means that no one may raise claims that she refuses to grant to others (reciprocity of contents) and that no one may simply assume that others share her own evaluative conceptions and interests so that she could claim to speak in their name or in the name of higher values (reciprocity of reasons). Finally, nobody may be excluded from the community of justification either (generality)."[1] However, standards of justification may vary in strength and demandingness, from mere *acceptance* (nonrejection), to *endorsement* or affirmation, to *identification*. This last requirement implies that one could not see oneself other than as an agent guided by such norms, while the first merely requires that one lacks reasons to reject the justification.

Further, variations can be found in the paths by which norms are justified, in that different forms of argumentation (what Forst calls "justification narratives") can produce the same result.[2] One might accept such a result but for reasons different from (though perhaps consistent with) those set forth by one's fellow citizens. Rawls's overlapping consensus spells out such a set of multiple paths to similar conclusions (principles of justice), and he proposes that this can be accomplished by way of public reason.[3] Although this is called a consensus, it is important to realize how an acceptance of *dissensus* is a crucial part of the picture, for I can (indeed must) accept deep and abiding differences with fellow citizens regarding the justificatory narrative that establishes the validity of those principles for them. However, Rawls also insists that our various comprehensive conceptions—our moral outlooks—must contain normative commitments to freedom and equality in order for justice to be established; these are values that we simply inherit (if we do) as part of the legacy of our political culture.[4]

Be that as it may, for norms to achieve a level of justification that can be stable—that can reproduce itself and, as Rawls puts it, generate its own support—there must be a connection between each of our ethical identities (or particular value commitments) and the justification narratives that we produce and share with our cocitizens.

Now, for finite beings beset by limitations of time, information, and any number of biases (cognitive and otherwise), one might forego the requirement that full-scale identification with what reason demands is constitutive of the moral perspective. One can accept the reasons that one considers subject to revisability under more ideal circumstances. And "accept" here can be understood as the weaker "cannot reasonably reject"—a formulation favored by Forst following Thomas Scanlon (and in some passages, John Rawls).[5] However, I will suggest in the following section that such identification must be available in some form if these justificatory practices are to be consistent with people's personal autonomy.[6] Before getting to that question, let us pause to consider what autonomy generally involves and look closely at those elements of self-government that emerge as focal points in our inquiry.

2. AUTONOMY

To govern oneself is to live in a way that reflects one's own values and perspective and not be coerced, manipulated, or rendered unable to make effective decisions about such values from that perspective. In this way, as I will explain in this section, autonomy involves a kind of self-justification, a capacity to endorse or accept the values and motives that guide one's life, whether those motives are generated internally or developed from social forces, teachers, parents, and so on and perhaps exercised in tandem with others with whom we closely identify. That is, without presupposing a controversial form of (hyper)individualism, self-government will in some way involve being in a position to legitimately accept one's decisions as one's own.

In the tradition of liberal political philosophy in which individual autonomy has played a central justificatory role, the condition of self-government has generally featured two components: independence from the undue influence of other persons or social trends in general and the positive capacity to generate and reflectively accept values of one's own. This first condition is associated with John Stuart Mill, whose comments on "individuality" (as one of the components of well-being) express this notion.[7] However, theorists in this tradition have more recently resisted this requirement as exemplifying a kind of hyperindividualism that a truly inclusive (and nonsexist) political philosophy should reject. Moreover, commentary by communitarians and multiculturalists has forced liberal theorists to reconsider the way in which autonomy must require *substantive* independence from connections with others, traditions, ethical frameworks, and so on.

This has led theorists who may or may not welcome the mantle of "liberal" but who emphasize autonomy in the normative architecture of their political philosophy to define that term in a way that maintains its normative status as foundational in a conception of democratic justice but is inclusive enough to include socially embedded and relationally defined selves.

Let us consider a sketch of such a notion, not to assume its final plausibility but to emphasize the nature and necessity of self-justification for autonomy.[8] Clearly, to be self-governing means at least having basic capacities for reflective decision-making. These include the basic capacities associated with will formation: the ability to form and execute intentions, construct action plans, and choose minimally rational means to carry them out. Such abilities should also include certain capacities for affective responsiveness—for example, the kind of empathy and care that would be required for a broad range of choices and roles, such as parenting and friendship, that require them. Without such conditions, the agent would lack the capacity to translate reflective apprehension of reasons into action; she would lack a fundamental component in an operative will.[9]

42

This captures what it means for an agent to act effectively, but autonomy requires further that the person acting is doing so out of an authentic ethical commitment—acting for her *own* reasons—and not merely in rote reaction to external forces. What is needed in addition, then, are conditions that specify when the values and motives that move a person's choices are authentically her own. Central to the account of such authenticity, I think, must be a model of the *self* as involved in the exercise of agency, specifically the contours of the agent that reflect what is *her*, as opposed to what happens to her or what is imposed on her. This is not to postulate an essential self that functions within an agent relative to which she can be self-realizing or self-developing. The (authentic) self at the center of autonomy can be understood procedurally as that set of functions and commitments that reflect a person's independent agency rather than her begrudging reactions to circumstance.

For these reasons, we need to be able to capture such a person's *perspective*, the particular way she has of leading her life. To understand this sort of evaluative orientation, we can make use of the concept of *practical identity*, following Christine Korsgaard but adapted in several ways. Practical identities, in Korsgaard's sense, are those self-descriptions under which one sees one's life as worth pursuing.[10] Such a self-schema can be characterized by a set of identity categories that carry with them core normative commitments. To be this or that type of person—a professor, a parent, or a friend—is to be committed to a set of values that provide reasons to act in particular ways. I would insist, further, that such identities be understood diachronically, in that they can only be conceived over a span of time that makes sense of memories and organizes future plans.[11]

In addition, practical identities guide our reflective evaluations in this way, and as such they do more than provide a propositional basis for arguments in support of our lower-order judgments, such as our decisions to treat particular desires as action guiding. Practical identities do perform this function—for example, when we articulate the commitments constitutive of our identities in propositional form and then use them in a practical syllogism justifying our decisions. But more than this, basic commitments of this sort perform what we can call an *orienting* function: they order the moral world in a way that sets the stage for our evaluations themselves.[12]

This functional feature of practical identities is important in understanding how they can speak for the agent, for without this understanding of the functioning self—the "I-self" in William James's terminology—autonomy would not mark the quality of agency that grounds judgments of responsibility, praise, and blame; nor would it indicate why the autonomous agent is the locus of discursive interchange involved in normative justification. This functioning self expresses the individually unique perspective that others recognize and react to as *this* concrete person (even if the self in question is thoroughly socially defined).

43

Other features of practical identities ground this point further: first, one's practical identity structures and guides reflection so that when we consider our motives and decisions, we do so in a way that manifests our basic commitments. Such identities explain and rationalize our motives over a variety of conditions and over time. Practical identities also organize memory, in that having a working self-concept structured by value commitments of this sort is necessary to engage in the active construction of narrative first-person memories.

In addition, contexts where collective deliberation is called for— group decision-making—operate in ways that assume participants are able to speak for themselves. Different voices are taken seriously as equal members of the group dynamic precisely because, it is assumed, they represent a unique perspective that is their own and not merely a manipulated or implanted viewpoint imposed on them. Utilizing a practical perspective/identity allows persons to represent themselves in such interpersonal interactions.

So in the view sketched here, a person is autonomous if, from the perspective of her diachronic practical identity, she can reflectively accept her motives given her history and social condition. By "accept" here, I mean fit into an intelligible personal narrative that consistently guides her actions and grounds her reasons for acting without alienation. And by "alienation," I mean feelings of self-abnegation, deep and painful conflict, and internal resistance.[13]

This is important, for it touches on the question of how much self-justification is involved in self-government. To be autonomous, is it necessary to think, explicitly, that one's basic values are grounded in unassailable foundations and supported by flawless argumentation? This is doubtful. First, there is the obvious fact that much activity that clearly is attributable to the agent herself is undertaken automatically, passionately, or with an immediate commitment that leaves no room for reflective consideration. The autonomous person has the *capacity* to reflect and is disposed to reflectively accept her actions and the values supporting them, but she may not explicitly do so in many cases. What matters is that she is not alienated in forming and acting on her intentions grounded in her diachronic identity.

But how can this be? Can one really be self-governing if one is ambivalent about one's reasons for action?[14] The test for autonomy, I think, is that one's practical commitments enable one to engage in the recursive self-generation of reasons for action. What I mean by this is that one is able to act on reasons that emerge from a practical perspective that, recursively, provide further, ongoing reasons to continue such action. The fact that I did something earlier that emanated from my perspective then—and I don't currently have reason to change my mind—independently provides me with an ongoing reason to continue acting in this way. Lacking alienation, in the sense I've described, is sufficient as a level of commitment to enable this recursive motivational grounding for action.[15]

This requirement of recursive reason-generation connects with what many have stressed in accounts of autonomy—namely, relational, social, or interpersonal conditions for autonomy. These have ranged from constitutive conditions such as mutual recognition to contingent requirements of access to supportive social systems and caring relations. One such condition that we must emphasize is *self-trust* and the acknowledgment by others of one's own normative authority.[16] Such self-trust or sense of basic agential competence is required for autonomous agency to function as recursively reason giving. By that I mean that reflectively endorsed actions partly constitute the life of the agent, and seeing oneself as the kind of person who does those kinds of things will, in the normal case, provide one with reasons to continue with the plan exemplified by those actions and decisions. Self-trust (or in a more Kantian register, self-respect) names the condition of seeing oneself as a self-validating source of claims that one makes on one's future self. In this further way, we see the essential diachronicity (or historicity) of agency.

45

Finally, one other dimension of this model that bears emphasis is that it views the self of self-government in sociohistorical terms. That is to say, agents are understood as occupying identities that make essential reference to other persons, practices, traditions, and relations that mark their social milieu. Without sustained connections with those social elements of the sort that support the reflective generation of reasons to act according to such an identity, the person would experience alienation of the sort that undercuts autonomy. Forst makes a parallel point at the social level when he writes, "Justification narratives develop normative power to the extent that they cast the political and social world in a certain light, connect the past, present, and future, reality and ideals, as well as individuals and a collective, and form them into an accepted order of justification."[17] As I said, a person's authentic practical identity bears the marks of her past, in that it is structured as a diachronically functioning mechanism that guides action over time in terms of plans and projects that extend indefinitely into the future and that orient memory (and by extension pride, guilt, regret, and shame). One's orientation toward one's past actions speaks to the ways in which one might maintain ongoing reflective self-government either by an acceptance of those actions (and treatment from others) or in a healthy regret and atonement for one's failings. When retrospective judgment serves to undercut the current effectiveness of one's practical identity—when one's sense of self-trust is deflated because of the stains of past experiences—then one is in serious danger of losing an ongoing capacity for autonomy. Certain pathologies and neuroses exemplify such failures. This point will be of special importance in what follows.

I have gone into detail about these components of autonomy not to defend the final plausibility of such a model (though I hope these are relatively uncontroversial) but to emphasize elements of self-governing agency that will bring into focus the connection between such agency and interpersonal respect. What matters in the present context is how autonomy can function in the interpersonal confrontations that the right to justification involves, for on that view, one must respond to such a right in terms that resonate with the self-justification implicit in autonomy, respect for which is expressed in exercising that right.

46

3. FROM SELF- TO SOCIAL JUSTIFICATION: AUTONOMY AND JUSTICE

In the project of critically appraising the function and prospects of liberal democracies and in establishing the requirements of justice for such polities, we must ask how practices and institutions at the social level can be legitimated for persons who view themselves as free (autonomous in my sense) and equal members of society. Following Forst, we can say that the justification of norms governing such practices and institutions must meet the criteria of reciprocity and generality, at least at a first pass, for persons who are themselves thoroughly embedded in ethical lifeworlds that are highly variegated and complex. Equally important is the acknowledgment that the social settings in which this critical appraisal takes place are rife with a history and ongoing practice of domination and victimization, such that we engage very much in a kind of nonideal theorizing in raising questions of justice.

I follow Forst in seeing political legitimacy (as the fundamental requirement of justice for institutions) as established through *procedural* specifications that make possible ongoing public discourse for a multidimensionally diverse populace. The moral duty to fulfill others' right to justification translates into a political imperative that, for Forst, allows for the structuring and ongoing operation of deliberative, democratic mechanisms of public will formation.

Such procedural specifications allow for a form of political liberty for citizens that aims to protect their autonomy along several vectors, specifically involving moral, ethical, legal, political, and social self-government.[18] As he puts it, "The relation between moral, ethical, and legal autonomy within a concept of political liberty necessitates the following step: the principle of reciprocal and general justification must be translated into procedures of 'public justification' among citizens as the authors of the law."[19] Parties to this justificatory exchange are those reasonable persons engaged in reciprocal and general practices of justification itself. As Forst wrote, "The justifying reasons . . . must be those that would be reasonably acceptable to persons in general. . . . The 'community of justification' in moral matters is the community of all human beings as moral persons, and those concretely affected are, as representatives of this community so to speak, the primary addressees of justification."[20] Put another way, both the one offering the justification and those accepting it as valid are considered as autonomous moral beings.

This connects with Forst's well-developed moral theorizing according to which practical reason grounds moral justification and this form of reasoning is self-motivating. That is, "to be part of a social practice means understanding its rules and hence its point; and to see the point of the practice of moral justification means *accepting* the principle that I owe this justification to every moral person equally, *independently* of any prior performance on their part and independently of my ethical preferences."[21] However, in order for persons reasoning in this way to maintain their autonomy, it must be the case (as Forst assumes) that as practical agents, they *identify* with the demands of justification so spelled out—in other words, only insofar as the being who is defined by a commitment to unconditional duty as part of that person's practical identity can follow the moral law in this form and thus manifest obedience to a law one gives to *oneself*. Otherwise, obligations purportedly grounded in an impersonal viewpoint can be quite alien. For autonomy to be consistent with moral duty, the perspective in which such duty is justified is one that the agent identifies with. This is, of course, the view famously developed in Immanuel Kant that "the will is not merely subject to the law but subject to it in such a way that it must be viewed as also giving the laws to itself and just because of this as first subject to the law (of which it can regard itself as the author)."[22]

However, this assumption is, of course, highly controversial. That is, it cannot merely be assumed that one's socially structured practical identity will simply coincide with the impersonally grounded moral law, although Forst himself and other Kantians have done much to make such a view plausible.[23] While I will not pursue this issue here, it must at least be admitted at this point that in a social world of reasonable but radically diverging moral outlooks, the claim that interpersonal justification aligns with intrapersonal self-government cannot simply be postulated based on an identification between the personal and the ethical.

Before moving on, let me add an observation about the alleged priority of the requirements of justice over the impetus to promote the good, for this will bear on our question of whether people's government of themselves by way of their commitment to ethical values squares with the need to justify themselves to others.

As Forst acknowledges, the traditional independence of conceptions of the right from conceptions of the good has been roundly misunderstood and, in a different way, exaggerated.

Traditional liberal political thought places a strict priority on principles of justice—the right—over advancing the social (or individual) good. However, this simplified picture of liberal justice is clearly somewhat of a caricature. Rawls, for example, talks about the priority of right *and* conceptions of the good, not the absolute priority of the first over the second but a complementarity that allows for the formal demands of justice to be motivating for persons who have their own self-guiding purposes.[24]

Even outside of the narrow purview of standard liberal theory, models of democratic justice view rights protections as part of a network of just practices and institutions that include obligations to promote those social and individual goods that are inherent in those democratic practices. There is nothing, then, about the focus on individual rights that requires the promotion of social goods be relegated to a secondary status. Indeed, I would stress that the collective promotion of goods such as positive freedom and (socially structured) autonomy is co-original (as Habermas puts it) with erecting rights-protecting legal institutions of democratic self-government.[25]

For Forst, the requirements of procedural integrity of reciprocal and general reason giving support substantive commitments such as the equal value of all participants, though that commitment is not a value or a virtue independent of the procedural requirements of fair reason giving itself.[26] This point also arises in Forst's discussion of the requirements of social support for deliberative democracy, which in part constitutes practices of justification as he envisions them. Democratic practices require social and cultural supports, which, in turn, assume and promote people's commitment to ethical values and ends.[27]

Forst develops this idea in claiming that sufficiently reproducible and stable practices of justification will require citizens to develop and maintain a sense of mutual trust and commitment to a shared conception of justice. He writes, "The basis of such a supportive culture, then, has to be a *shared sense of justice* that tells citizens what they owe to one another on moral grounds as members of their shared basic social structure."[28] This commitment entails a kind of responsibility on the part of citizens that is "based on a contextualized . . . sense of justice [and constitutes] the core of an ethos of democracy that integrates a political community normatively as a 'community of responsibility.' In that way, relations of political *trust* can evolve between citizens."[29] In a vein echoing Rawls's political conception but also departing from it, Forst suggests (regarding the cultural conditions for deliberative democracy again) that "a middle way is needed between liberal conceptions like the 'overlapping consensus' and the communitarian ideals of a *substantielle Sittlichkeit*."[30] Forst developed such a middle ground throughout his work, from *Contexts of Justice* to the present day.[31] What I would like to do, however, is explore the required links between the formal structure of justice and commitments to ethical values of this sort through the lens of individual autonomy shaped earlier. In so doing, I will show how certain unresolved (perhaps unresolvable) challenges present themselves for such a project in the present social context.

4. AUTONOMY AND JUSTICE IN A NONIDEAL WORLD

To summarize what we've established so far, political legitimacy requires a commitment to reciprocal and general justification, which is linked to social and institutional practices that facilitate public discourse (democracy) and negotiation of difference. For such practices to have a point as well as maintain themselves from one generation to the next, certain elements of a conception of the good must also be posited as derivative complements to the requirements of justice. These include the value of justice (so conceived) itself, mutual trust and respect among citizens as equal and autonomous coparticipants in these discursive practices, and a general identification on the part of citizens with the conception of justice manifest in these practices. Hence justice requires a shared commitment to—and some manner of identification with—the procedural practices of mutual justification as well as an interpersonal sense of trust and cooperation that these procedures presuppose.

A question we raised earlier about such interpersonal practices of justification concerned the stringency and mode that such justification needs to take for it to perform its normative function. Another way to raise this issue is to ask, How idealized is the picture of agents participating in these practices of justification? How independent are they conceived to be from the kinds of errors, biases, myopias, and obsessions that plague us all and that profoundly mark the social worlds we inhabit?

This same issue arises at the level of individual autonomy in a way that may be informative here, for the model I laid out assumes that the first-person perspective of an individual, reflecting on her motives in light of her history and her own social connectedness, is authoritative in securing her self-government. That is, the central requirement of autonomy is that a person be able to reflectively accept *herself* through the lens of her diachronic practical identity. This identity is marked by her actual past, and indeed her reflections must make sense of that past and orient her in light of it. Or not, in which case her failure may well mark a lack of autonomy, from radical disorientation, trauma, or lack of social support sufficient to ward off this kind of internal alienation.

But, of course, to utter a truism bordering on the banal, none of us is perfect. In fact, we are quite predictably imperfect, full of cognitive biases, a penchant for self-serving rationalizations, suppressions of dissonant thoughts and motivations, and so on. We are boringly predictable in our failures. So we might ask, on the question of what are our authentic, self-governing motives and values, Why take our words for it?

There are various answers one might give to such questions. One is epistemic. This was given first in this context by J. S. Mill—namely, that while we are terrible judges of our own motivations, we are, generally speaking, better than anyone else. In practical situations where complexities of interpretation, aim, motive, and social context are in evidence, onlookers or impersonal social agencies will lack the perspective and information to determine our motives and values that we have (albeit flawed) access to. As Mill put it, "With respect to his own feelings and circumstances, the most ordinary man or woman has means of knowledge immeasurably surpassing those that can be possessed by any one else."[32]

51

But this sort of contingent speculation is weak compared to the relatively unconditional respect required for the autonomous agent's standing as a general authority over her values and aims.[33] A stronger grounding for such first-person authority is what can be called the normative argument—namely, that the nature of practical reason itself and the demands of interpersonal respect that morality imposes require that persons be afforded the final say in determining and representing their own motives.[34]

We can understand this strategy by recalling the phenomenon of self-trust I noted in my discussion of autonomy. I noted there that self-reflection through the functionality of a diachronic practical identity provides a recursive and reflexive endorsement of the very operation of this identity. That is, the crucial functional aspect of practical identities is that they are able to provide reasons for acts and continuation of action plans. Only if the feedback mechanism of reflexive self-affirmation is functioning can such identities play this reason-giving role.

When one acts from reasons grounded in one's practical identity and succeeds in achieving a desired end, a sense of satisfaction results as well as a judgment that such a sequence was worth doing. If one is frustrated in one's attempt, regret ensues. If one's actions have a moral character, one feels moral satisfaction from his success and guilt or shame from his failure. Self-affirming feedback mechanisms underlie these reactions: satisfaction from acting out an identity one feels is worth having or frustration and regret at failing to live up to the expectations of that identity. Note that these simple vectors of reaction describe typical deliberative action, which links reasons and motives.

52 Only if this recursive mechanism functions in something like this manner will one have *continued* reason and motive to act from the practical identity that frames deliberation and choice. This self-trust, then, translates into interpersonal respect in that the very activity of a practical agent depends on having such confidence (despite our admittedly glaring failures), and so social interaction guided by a respect for another's autonomous agency must proceed via a parallel form of acknowledging the normative authority of the other concerning her own intentions.

Where does that leave us, then, in our inquiries into the interaction between the intrapersonal demands of autonomy and the interpersonal demands of justification? As I noted, autonomous agency should be understood as historically structured, such that ongoing reflective self-acceptance must come to terms with our personal histories. This involves accepting oneself through the lens of one's diachronic practical identity in ways that make sense of both the past and the future. The self-justification involved here need not reach to the level of foundational justification but merely a degree of self-acceptance (nonalienation) that allows for recursive, ongoing reason giving (self-trust). This involves accepting the values that define one's life as an individual and also as a social being with intersubjective elements of one's identity, social roles, and aspirations.

Further, for autonomy in this sense to be enjoyed and also respected by others, citizens must affirm the publicly promoted values that are inherent in the practices of justification at the social and political levels. That is, the commitment to a public conception of the good is complementary to the requirements of political legitimacy, which for our purposes amounts to the practices of reciprocal and general justification of the legal and social norms shaping people's lives. This level of identification with such public values, however, need only match the kind of intrapersonal self-justification just described, affirmation to a degree that allows for an ongoing motivated commitment to their demands, on the order of the recursive reason giving that individual autonomy requires. So social and political practices of public justification must operate in a way that allows participants to accept them from the point of view of their own practical identities. Failure to secure such acceptance would drive a wedge between the demands of justice (as we, following Forst, conceive it) and respect for autonomy.

However, all this must be posited for a world where past and ongoing *injustices* are everywhere in evidence. This last component of my analysis poses the greatest challenge for this vision, as it forces us to confront the sociological conditions where such social trust is so often lacking. That is, we must emphasize the nonideal social conditions to which these demands for justification are to be enacted. As Forst puts a similar point, critical theory "starts from an analysis of the *real* relations of subjugation in order to develop a 'grounded' conception of critical justice."[35] Justice is not utopian, though it is morally grounded, but normative for all agents who live in social landscapes marked by radical inequalities of power.

Similarly, social values and practices that mark the ethical dimensions of a given society (or social location) bear the marks of the injustices and pathologies of its own past. In so-called liberal democracies such as the United States, for example, lip service has been paid for generations to the freedom and equality of citizens while institutionally undercutting such values for millions of its citizens through patriarchal legal structures, slavery and Jim Crow, racially motivated practices of mass incarceration, and the tolerance of ubiquitous patterns of sexual violence. Confrontations between contemporary citizens engaged in the practice of reciprocal justification will reflect that history—we all have blood on our clothes, either from our crimes or from our scars. And the attitudes brought to bear on that history will determine the degree of self-trust required for stable practices of mutual justification to function.

The question arises, then, of how the minimal degree of mutual identification with shared or sharable social aims can get a foothold in a social setting marked, as they all are, by such rampant violations of trust in the past. When the systematic breakdown of public trust in governmental institutions and social practices of fellow citizens is in evidence, then even the minimal identification required for self-government to match the requirements of public justification is lacking. For individual autonomy to be consistent with the requirements of public justification of the sort Forst's view requires, there must be a sense of public trust in the procedural integrity of the social and political institutions of one's society. Without such trust, requiring citizens to participate in and be guided by the processes of justification (and the corresponding generation of laws) is to impose an alien force upon them and to fail to respect their autonomy.

However, this potential conflict should not be overdrawn, for remember that in my analysis of the parallel demands of intra- and interpersonal justification (autonomy and justice), I argued that individual autonomy required reflective self-*acceptance* to a degree that allowed the ongoing, reciprocal self-trust needed for diachronically structured reason giving. This is far short of requiring all-out self-justification without qualification. But it does require that the personal ethical commitments that define the identities of citizens contain within them *social* commitments to the values that are inherent in the processes of public justification. This view is weaker than the wholesale identification with the moral law—and the impersonal point of view that generates it—and as such is weaker than the brand of Kantianism that Forst defends. But while I have not argued directly against that Kantian picture, I have suggested that in a world marked by wholesale victimization and widespread mistrust of social institutions (given their past), such impersonal identification and shared moral commitment may well be too much to ask.

5. CONCLUSION

What I have attempted here is to investigate the parallel requirements and challenges of individual and collective self-government. That is, the demands of reciprocal and general justification, especially instantiated in social practices and political institutions, mirror the requirements of personal autonomy for which such practices of justification show respect. I argued that a complementarity must be established between the formal desiderata of justification with the substantive ethical values inherent in its operation, including trust and identification with the normativity of the process itself. And I noted how the imperfections of our social worlds make establishing such complementarity doubly challenging, though I suggested (albeit without much direct argument) that such a complementarity does not require citizens' personal com- 55 mitment to an impersonal (Kantian) moral point of view but merely an overlap between persons' ethical commitments and the values inherent in the social practices of justification, the chief of which is social trust in participants in those practices and institutions. The history of exclusion, violence, and injustice that marks all real-world institutions that pretend to meet these requirements underscores the severity of such a challenge.

Whether such challenges can be met is left an open question here, but it is one that is not meant to undercut the profound power of the vision of justice and social critique offered by Rainer Forst in his far-reaching and deeply important philosophical work.

NOTES

1. Rainer Forst, *Normativity and Power: Analyzing Social Orders of Justification,* trans. Ciaran Cronin (Oxford: Oxford University Press, 2017), 4:43.
2. Ibid., chap. 3.
3. John Rawls, *The Law of Peoples: With the Idea of Public Reason Revisited* (Cambridge: Harvard University Press, 1999), 129–80.
4. John Rawls, *Political Liberalism* (New York: Columbia University Press, 1993), 133–72, Lec. IV.
5. Forst, *Normativity and Power;* T. M. Scanlon, *What We Owe to Each Other* (Cambridge: Harvard University Press, 1998).
6. Moral justification in this vein can be contrasted with ethical commitment, as explicated by Forst. Ethical commitment refers to the values inherent in social practices and ways of life that define identities at the individual and community level. Such commitments are fundamental to the social self-conceptions of agents for Forst, but the requirements of moral justification always rise above, so to speak, any such first-order value orientations. In contrast to ethical values, he writes, the validity claim of moral norms is not "That is good for me" but instead "That is what is morally required as something valid for every person in a recip-rocal and general way" (Forst, *Normativity and Power,* 42). Moral norms must motivate categorically, without ethical support. For a sustained discussion of this contrast, see Rainer Forst, *The Right to Justification: Elements of a Constructivist Theory of Justice* (New York: Columbia University Press, 2007), chap. 3.
7. See John Stuart Mill, *On Liberty,* ed. David Spitz (New York: Norton, 1975), chap. 3.

8. What follows is a brief and revised version of the view I develop in *The Politics of Persons: Individual Autonomy and Socio-historical Selves* (Cambridge: Cambridge University Press, 2009). See also my "Anti-perfectionism and Autonomy in an Imperfect World: Comments on Joseph Raz's *The Morality of Freedom* 30 Years On," forthcoming in *Moral Philosophy and Politics.*

56

9. This is true not only for one to *succeed* in pursuing these role-defined pursuits but for one to undertake them in the first place. One cannot *be* a mother or a friend (under modern conditions) if one lacks any capacity for empathy and care for significant others. Moreover, there will be certain sorts of social and interpersonal *relations* that will be required for a person to develop the kinds of deliberative and choice-making capacities that autonomy requires. Not only a caring and supportive upbringing but ongoing relations of respect for one's normative authority will be required for a person to function as an effective decision-maker in many or most contexts. Note, however, that the relational conditions I refer to here are not inherently required for self-governing agency (as some have claimed) as, for example, would be required by a Hegelian conception of the subject in which interpersonal recognition in part *constitutes* self-governing agency. Rather, my view is that such relational dynamics are *contingently* related to the core capabilities of deliberation and effective choice named in the model because they are, generally speaking, instrumentally necessary for them (the core capabilities) to function. See, e.g., Catriona Mackenzie, "Relational Autonomy, Normative Authority and Perfectionism," *Journal of Social Philosophy* 39, no. 4 (2008): 512–33.

10. See Christine Korsgaard, *The Sources of Normativity* (Cambridge: Cambridge University Press, 1996).

11. This point echoes one of the central features of Michael Bratman's "planning" model of agency; see Michael Bratman, *Structures of Agency: Essays* (Oxford: Oxford University Press, 2007).

12. This is akin to what Barbara Herman called "rules of moral salience." See Herman, "The Practice of Moral Judgment," *Journal of Philosophy* 82, no. 8 (1985): 414–36.

13. For further development of this idea of alienation, see "Decentered Social Selves: Interrogating Alienation in Conversation with Rahel Jaeggi," in *From Alienation to Forms of Life: The Critical Theory of Rahel Jaeggi*, ed. Amy Allen and Eduardo Mendieta (University Park: Pennsylvania State University Press, 2018), 41–58.

14. Cf. Michael Bratman's criticism of a similar aspect of Frankfurt's view: Bratman, *Faces of Intention: Selected Essays on Intention and Agency* (Cambridge: Cambridge University Press, 1999), 185–206. For discussion of Bratman's critique, see Christman, *Politics of Persons*, 145–46.

15. Again, the echoes of Bratman's planning model of agency are instructive. On Bratman's view, one acts intentionally and with self-governing agency when (among other things) one's acts fit with a partial plan that one has no reason to reject. See Bratman, *Structures of Agency.*

16. See, e.g., Keith Lehrer, *Self-Trust: A Study of Reason, Knowledge, and Autonomy* (Cambridge, MA: MIT Press, 2002); Trudy Grovier, "Self-Trust, Autonomy, and Self-Esteem," *Hypatia* 8, no. 1 (1993): 99–120.

17. Forst, *Normativity and Power*, 89. Elsewhere he adds, "We must understand the normativity of ethical justification in terms of a network of relations shaped by individual life decisions, but also by 'volitional necessities' in Harry Frankfurt's

sense—hence, by ethical valuations and relations that simply constitute me as the person I am" (ibid., 39).

18. See Rainer Forst, "Political Liberty: Integrating Five Conceptions of Autonomy," in *Autonomy and the Challenges to Liberalism: New Essays,* ed. John Christman and Joel Anderson (Cambridge: Cambridge University Press, 2005), 226–45 (reprinted in Forst, *Right to Justification,* chap. 5).

19. Forst, *Right to Justification,* 135.

20. Ibid., 19.

21. Ibid., 46.

22. Immanuel Kant, *Groundwork of the Metaphysics of Morals,* in *Immanuel Kant: Practical Philosophy,* trans. and ed. Mary Gregor (Cambridge: Cambridge University Press, 1996), 81.

23. See Forst, *Right to Justification,* part 1. See also Korsgaard, *Sources of Normativity.*

24. See Rawls, *Political Liberalism,* 173–211, Lec. V.

25. See Jürgen Habermas, *Between Facts and Norms* (Cambridge, MA: MIT Press, 1996), sec. 3.1.

26. Forst, *Right to Justification,* 185.

27. Ibid., 182–83.

28. Ibid., 179.

29. Ibid., 180.

30. Ibid., 178.

31. Rainer Forst, *Contexts of Justice: Political Philosophy Beyond Liberalism and Communitarianism,* trans. John M. M. Farrell (Berkeley: University of Californian Press, 1994).

32. Mill, *On Liberty,* 71.

33. Cf. Richard Thaler and Cass Sunstein, *Nudge* (New York: Penguin, 2008); Sarah Conly, *Against Autonomy: Justifying Coercive Paternalism* (Cambridge: Cambridge University Press, 2013).

34. Further elaboration of this issue occurs in my "Decentered Social Selves." The next two paragraphs are adapted from that discussion.

35. Forst, *Normativity and Power,* 22.

CHAPTER 4

Objectionable Objections

On Toleration, Respect, and Esteem

Mattias Iser

1. INTRODUCTION

Complex modern societies are characterized by a pluralism of cultures and worldviews. For that reason, toleration is regarded as an important political virtue. It is generally agreed that to tolerate means to accept something that one objects to as "false or bad"[1] or as something to be "condemned."[2] From the perspective of those tolerated, being objected to or even condemned is highly problematic, since they presumably cannot share the reasons for it. This frequently gives rise to the claim that one ought to move beyond toleration in order to achieve a fully just society. Rainer Forst disagrees. He has developed one of the most intriguing and demanding accounts of toleration, in which he argues that such a claim reacts to the historically influential, but mistaken, "permission" conception. According to it, a powerful group grants the less powerful group the permission to hold on to views or engage in practices under certain conditions although the powerful group finds them objectionable. Such permission defines the realm of toleration in a one-sided manner and can in principle be revoked at any time. It is thus a paradigmatic form of domination that expresses unequal status.

However, if societies and their citizens are guided by the alternative "respect" conception, this deep ambivalence vanishes. Now two groups mutually ascribe to each other the *right* to hold views or engage in practices even if they object to each other's perspective. They do so properly if they realize that the reasons for such acceptance are of a higher order than those for their objections. Whereas the latter are merely grounded in a particular conception of the good, which cannot be shown to be categorically binding in the strong sense of reciprocal and general non-rejectability,[3] the former express the morally fundamental respect for the other as an agent with a right to justification and an acknowledgment of large areas of reasonable disagreement. This moral acceptance rules out any legal enactment of the ethical objection so as to coerce the other, but it does not cancel out the objection itself. Only if one can show that the aspect objected to is morally wrong should it also be rejected—that is, legally and morally prohibited.[4] Accordingly, for Forst, tolerant persons have to be "context virtuosi."[5] By embracing the respect conception, Forst also distances himself from the "esteem" conception that demands that we should value other lifestyles or cultures, even if only partly, on the basis of ethical values.[6] This, he claims, cannot be required by justice: "This is what the respect conception implies: equal rights for identities even though some of them are not just viewed as 'different' but also objected to by social majorities—as long as such an objection is insufficient to justify a rejection by law."[7] In what follows, I argue that Forst's respect conception might allow for too many objections being held in a wrong way. The question whether a view is too permissive in this regard becomes salient once one considers the negative impact that objections of a certain kind, especially condemnations, can have on those against whom they are held—and perhaps even publicly expressed. In order to make more vivid what is at stake, I will provide the example of a fictitious society called *Enlightened Despisistan* in section 2. Although it is enlightened in that its citizens affirm the respect conception, its salient feature is that the majority strongly objects to most if not all "ethical" beliefs or practices of the minority. They object so strongly that they end up despising the minority. This example highlights what is problematic with a narrow reading of the respect conception. Forst seems to share at least some of my worries, and thus, in section 3, I lay out how he normatively restricts the set of unobjectionable objections. However, the way he does this raises an important question to be discussed in section 4: Why is it necessary to restrict the objection component at all, if Forst sees the main work of toleration as consisting in drawing a clear demarcation between objection on the one hand and acceptance and rejection on the other? Here I will argue that one cannot explain our desire to restrict the objection component without taking the dimension of esteem into account because some forms of injustice do not show proper respect exactly because due esteem is withheld. Finally, in section 5, I will propose an imperfect duty of esteem learning,[8] which in one reading is already implicit in Forst's very idea of a fundamental right of justification. However, as he does not make it explicit, I take it to be an important addition to his respect conception, which, I am claiming, should take on elements of the esteem conception without being grounded in esteem.

2. A FICTITIOUS EXAMPLE: *ENLIGHTENED DESPISISTAN*

Imagine a society in which everyone is accorded equal rights and liberties as well as equal opportunities. Even if they do not excel in a career, their basic income guarantees that they can make proper use of their legal rights, including their right to participate in democratic processes of will-formation. What is more, this society attempts to realize state neutrality. All this flows from a fundamental respect for the other as a member of humanity or a citizen of the political order. This certainly sounds like a very desirable political order. However, there is a caveat. The wider society—or perhaps, rather, the majority culture[9]—objects to most if not all of what a minority culture is doing and believing.[10]

Yet objections come in different shapes and sizes. Frequently, we disagree with others—and thus object to their views—without caring too much. We might even regard our disagreement as productive, especially within a deliberative democracy, and thus cherish the diversity of cultures that leads to such reasonable disagreement. Objections that are relevant for the issue of toleration seem to be of a different kind. They have to be considered serious enough to raise the question of whether the view or practice objected to should be prohibited— otherwise the question of whether acceptance due to respect ought to trump the ethical objection would not arise. In the fictitious society I am imagining, this takes another turn to the extreme. Members of the majority culture do not merely object; they deeply despise the views and practices they are tolerating. Perhaps they even express this publicly, either by voicing it in informal conversations that members of the minority will frequently overhear or by ways of reacting, for instance, by certain gestures or facial expressions to members of the minority witness on the street. They might do so explicitly through the media or even within parliament in order to convince members of the minority to change their ways. Thus *Enlightened Despisistan* is an extreme case with regard to both the breadth and the intensity with which objections are held. But as spelled out earlier, this society is crucially different from *Unenlightened Despisistan,* which was its historical forerunner, by embracing the respect conception. The majority might argue that members of the minority are free to find their way of living repugnant as well (although one might sense a certain unfairness in the fact that they are the majority culture, after all).

Perhaps there is nothing to lament about *Enlightened Despisistan.* However, if one finds fault with such a respectfully tolerant society, the question is why. It is important to stress that the problem does not lie in the political or legal but in the cultural sphere. Thus, of the five dimensions of a tolerant society that Forst distinguishes, two are of special salience for the topic at hand: first, the toleration "between citizens as individuals," especially with regard to, second, the "space of toleration" that consists of nonlegal "norms and understandings."[11] Forst, in contrast, highlights the toleration between citizens as individuals primarily with regard to, third, the "tolerance of the legal norms themselves" and, fourth, the "tolerance of the political system and its institutions."[12] Finally, talk of the "tolerance of the state"[13] should be avoided as this would signal that the state, understood as an actor, objects to certain practices, whereas it ought to be a neutral arbiter. Within the third and fourth dimensions, the difference between ethical objection and legal acceptance can be made most clearly. What, however, would moral acceptance imply with regard to cultural norms and understandings one ethically objects to? Forst, here very much in the tradition of critical theory, admits that "not only are political-legal practical constraints in need of justification but also intersubjective constraints on action in general; the latter even constitute the normal case in moral interactions."[14] However, it remains to be spelled out what a moral constraint on action beyond the legal realm amounts to. If subject A objects to subject B's actions and condemns them, that condemnation seems to be exactly the sanction that morality has on offer. Perhaps Forst asks A to restrain her condemnation in acknowledgment that it is only ethical and not moral. But it remains unclear how A would have to change her ways of condemning. A radical version would require of the objecting agent not even to express such objection as a condemnation. However, Forst is rather adamant that relativizing one's objections as ethical does not commit one to holding them to be less true or less certain. Although the tolerant person has to identify with the moral demands that trump her objections, the ethical objection remains untouched as "moral responsibility is one thing, ethically embracing it another. Tolerance may be perceived simultaneously as a reinforcement of the self and as an affront of the self."[15] This picture of a tension-stricken individual is intriguing and may often be appropriate. But it also might make it too easy for persons to cling to their harmful objections by insisting on their own ethical beliefs. Thus there seems to be the danger of allowing too many objectionable objections. Everything depends on the question of what morally "curbing"[16] our ethical convictions actually entails and whether *Enlightened Despisistan* would hereby be ruled out.

A passage by John Stuart Mill might serve as a warning. Although unyielding in emphasizing the crucial dangers of not only legal but social norms that suppress idiosyncratic deviations, he believes that voicing contempt at features that do not do any harm to someone else but are objectively "debased" is permissible:

> There is a degree of folly [. . .] which [. . .] renders him
> necessarily and properly a subject of distaste, or, in extreme

cases, even of contempt. [...] We are not bound, for example, to seek his society; we have a right to avoid it (though not to parade the avoidance), for we have a right to choose the society most acceptable to us. We have a right, and it may be our duty, to caution others against him, if we think his example or conversation likely to have a pernicious effect on those with whom he associates. [...] In these various modes a person may suffer very severe penalties at the hands of others, for faults which directly concern only himself.[17]

Although Mill has different objections in mind than Forst does (namely, based on what he takes to be reciprocally and generally non-rejectable self-regarding duties), Mill's description renders visible how much nonlegal power the majority might hold even in *Enlightened Despisistan*—and that it is a power to harm. Forst might respond that such power is not illegitimate as long as it does not dominate (which does not seem to be the case in *Enlightened Despisistan*) or as long as the harm imposed is not wrongful (as in a justified critique or in voicing one's opinion under rights accorded by a just regime of freedom of speech).

But Forst also seems to entertain the view that the majority does not even have such power because minorities are not in need of the cultural esteem (or company) of the majority. Although he admits that persons need self-esteem, he believes that such esteem can sufficiently be generated within a particular group one associates with.

> Internal forms of recognition of this identity as generating sufficient self-esteem were the precondition of being able to fight at all; hence, what we find here is a struggle for recognition, which at the same time does not seem to be a struggle for the general social recognition or esteem of one's identity in a qualitative, Hegelian sense of *Sittlichkeit*. Rather, what was demanded was the freedom to keep one's identity as a communal one and to be recognized as equal legal and political citizens. . . . A certain communal and personal identity was the precondition, not the aim of the struggle for recognition.[18]

Although Forst is certainly right that, first, gaining respect has more political urgency than achieving esteem and frequently was the primary aim of progressive movements and that, second, it would be an exaggeration to say that self-esteem can only be generated if one is esteemed by the entire society, it is nonetheless implausible that already-existing self-esteem rules out that one would also struggle for esteem by the wider society. Members of a society partake not only in a shared political culture but also in a general "societal culture."[19] Axel Honneth has tried to argue for the importance of this perspective not least because every society is necessarily integrated by social spheres of mutual esteem.[20] If citizens depend for their self-understanding on the views of others with regard to at least parts of their identities, then insisting that they will get all they need from their specific community is misleading. That Forst at least shares some of my concerns becomes obvious once one turns to his views on objectionable objections.

3. FORST'S ACCOUNT OF OBJECTIONABLE OBJECTIONS

Whereas the acceptance and rejection components are fully determined by moral reasons, the objection component is not. At first sight, it seems to be up to the tolerant person what she objects to as long as she can clearly separate this ethical (or reasonably rejectable[21]) objection from a moral (or not reasonably rejectable) rejection.

But somewhat surprisingly, Forst admits that in some cases, one should not have certain objections. Even though, for Forst, objections do not have to be based on generally shareable reasons, "nevertheless certain criteria for a 'rational' critique are indispensable."[22] But what kind of "rational" critique is Forst envisioning here? At times, he follows John Horton in specifying the range of unobjectionable objections in a rather minimal fashion as not to be grounded on prejudice or blind hatred. Thus the racist, the homophobe, and the "narrow-minded bigot"[23] are ruled out. The exclusion of utterly baseless views seems to give rise to the demand of objections being "in a basic sense intersubjectively defensible."[24] Even though the tolerated person might not be able to share the reasons underlying the objection, she should at least be able to understand them as springing from reasoning that is not faulty or incoherent. This seems to be what her right of justification amounts to in this context. An unobjectionable objection has to be a "well-grounded ethical objection."[25] I take a well-grounded ethical objection to be one that makes sense within the worldview of the objecting agent. Thus if the agent does not apply her own worldview correctly or makes salient factual mistakes, it is not ethically well-grounded.

One has to remember, though, that neither well- nor ill-grounded views are, if reasonable disagreement prevails, convincing from within the worldview of the agent who is objected to. The belief of members of religion A that a specific religious practice of religion B is repugnant because it goes against God's will and thus the members of religion B will end up in hell might be "well-grounded" within the worldview of religion A. Or it might be based on a crucial misinterpretation of the holy text of religion A, which is not seen as authoritative by religion B. What kind of normative difference does it make? In both cases, the practices of members of religion B are objected to (perhaps even despised) and they cannot share the reasons. In addition, in both cases, the objections are trumped by moral considerations anyway so that they do not impact the (primarily legal) respect due to members of religion B.

Forst rightly harbors the intuition that there is something potentially harmful—and perhaps wrongfully harmful—about "unfounded" objections. He clearly sees the "danger of exerting repressive effects by perpetuating social discrimination and *baseless condemnations*,"[26] admitting that this is a "very important problem."[27] However, more has to be said about why exactly baseless objections should be overcome.

4. WHY ARE SOME OBJECTIONS OBJECTIONABLE?

Prejudices might be understood first and foremost as a failure to display an intellectual virtue—that is, of not to be utterly misguided in what one believes in. But why should this be an issue for toleration as a virtue of justice? The intellectual mistake must express something normatively worrisome or even an injustice—that is, either some form

65

of disrespect or an inappropriate lack of esteem. Forst seems to agree when he excludes "grossly irrational and immoral prejudices."[28] I take it that he has to interpret the holding of a prejudice as a matter of disrespect or, short of that, as a feature leading to disrespect. However, frequently it is also a matter of an inappropriate lack of esteem.

In what follows, I distinguish between an objection potentially being disrespectful or lacking in appropriate esteem (a) because of its content, (b) because of the way it was formed, and (c) because of the way it is expressed. Whereas Forst's critique of the tolerant racist seems to emphasize the dimension of content, the second dimension of how one forms one's objections is crucial for a theory highlighting the right and corresponding duty of justification. This duty entails, I argue in the next section, an imperfect duty to try to overcome one's objections as much as possible, especially in contexts where one knows them to be harmful.

a.

First, with regard to the content of an objection, does the belief of the tolerant racist in itself violate the condition of mutual respect, and is this the reason Forst explicitly rules out such prejudices? Objecting to the skin color or the origin of persons is especially baseless as the persons objected to cannot even react to the objection by changing their beliefs or practices. In comparison to such "intrinsic" racism, "extrinsic"[29] racism (or sexism) focuses on certain objectionable features that supposedly characterize the targeted group. Frequently, black people and women are described as inferior with regard to their moral beliefs and practices or simply as less capacious when it comes to specific skills. It is certainly the case that if such racism implies that the allegedly inferior race does not deserve the same respect in terms of rights and opportunities, then such an objection will be disrespectful in itself and might additionally lead to actions that will undermine a just basic structure manifesting equal respect.

But much depends on how one describes the tolerant racist. I simply assume that she embraces the respect conception (otherwise she would not pose a challenge for that conception).[30] At first glance,

Forst's respect conception seems to allow for someone holding the view that some races are inferior with regard to feature X without this implying any differential distribution of rights or opportunities. Under this description, the racist seems to do all that is required by the respect conception: she relativizes her own belief (and desire to act) because she recognizes the other person as demanding of respect. Many people believe that there are empirical differences between individual persons but that this should have no impact on their equal status because such a status is grounded not in differential esteem but in respect for our common humanity. By definition, the prejudice the racist holds then seems to be a matter of lacking esteem where esteem would be appropriate. If one mistakenly assigns someone a low level of intelligence or moral excellence, this is a mistake in the dimension of esteem, of accomplishment esteem in the former and moral esteem in the latter case. This seems to be the normative failure of the tolerant racist who embraces the respect conception.

A lack of appropriate esteem clearly constitutes an injustice where equality of opportunity is at stake—the basic normative principle of a meritocratic system of material and symbolic rewards. Here a lack of appropriate esteem transforms itself into a lack of just rewards. It is important to point out, though, that the following considerations about equal opportunity apply to any system of esteem that is factually in place in a society. In such a case, people can complain if they are not evaluated according to its criteria even if they do not share the validity of the criteria themselves. Beyond accomplishment esteem, any society that is built on certain moral convictions must have room for moral and political esteem (being especially tolerant should garner both kinds of esteem). Perhaps *Enlightened Despisistan*'s flaw is in not adequately appreciating these areas of human excellence in others that could at least counteract the negative attitudes harbored on the ethical level?

There are roughly two ways of how equality of opportunity can be undermined: First, the standard of esteem might itself be partial (being white is considered to be more beautiful than being black). Second, whether the standard itself is impartially justifiable (better-skilled surgeons should get higher pay) or not (belief in a God should be highly esteemed), the application of the standard can be partially or mistakenly carried out by, for instance, assuming that black surgeons will always be less skilled than white ones or that only Christians should be esteemed, hereby disregarding all other religions.

68   Such a misapplication is a case of both disrespect and lack of esteem. Imagine that two black candidates apply for a surgeon's position and the committee does not even look at the files. One candidate would get the job if looked at; the other is in fact unqualified. Both are disrespected in the sense that their right to due attention is violated because of racism—this is clearly covered by the respect conception. But the qualified person also suffers from a lack of due esteem given her credentials and the reigning esteem order. This is an additional injustice, but its content matter is that of withholding (accomplishment) esteem. I take it that the respect conception is supposed to cover such cases, especially via the criterion of reciprocal justification. However, this shows that esteem, also of the cultural kind, might be demandable. If you value X in your case, you also have to value it in mine. This might explain why Forst insists on objections being ethically well-grounded, so as to exclude applying different criteria to the other's view. This already points to the second dimension in which objections might be disrespectful or lacking appropriate esteem—namely, the way they are formed.

b.

How ought we to describe the normative failure of someone who holds on to a demeaning image of another despite contrary evidence? Is this disrespectful because she does not live up to her duty of justification? However, according to Forst, the duty of justification implies different criteria in different contexts. Certainly, this agent does not sufficiently care. But if the carelessness does not have any impact on the basic equality (including equal opportunity) that the basic structure has to guarantee, as the respect conception wants to ensure, one might wonder whether it should rather be described as a lack of esteem for the particular feature dismissed—which would amount to integrating elements of the esteem conception into one's account of toleration.

    In addition, as soon as one locates the normative problem on this level of belief formation, there may be cases where our judgments with regard to content and adequate formation do not align. Objections whose content is not objectionable might also be held without much thought and thus manifest insufficient care. Why would this not count as a normative failure? Even if an objection could be based on good reasons, the belief in its validity might be grounded on everything but these reasons. Thus one could argue that the content and the way of arriving at one's view must both be adequate in order to speak of unobjectionable objections.

69

But what exactly does "adequate" entail here? Objecting to someone from a mere whim or due to ill-founded prejudice appears to be clearly inadequate. This may be another reason Forst requires a well-founded ethical objection (i.e., trumped but not canceled out by moral acceptance) so that the agent being objected to can see that the objecting person has tried to direct sufficient attention to the problem at hand—an expression of due respect irrespective of how the tolerant person ends up judging what she tried to evaluate. However, for the objected person to find out whether she was disrespected will then involve evaluations of what counts as well-founded within the other's ethical conviction. For someone who does not share that ethical worldview, this might be hard to assess. But more important, the objection is directed against a view or practice that itself is immersed in an ethical worldview. So if one asks the objecting agent to construe a well-founded objection, it ought to be based not only on a good understanding of one's own comprehensive doctrine but also on a good understanding of the other's. All of this already points to a much more demanding idea of an imperfect duty of esteem learning, which I elaborate on in section 5. It is this duty that seems to be violated in *Enlightened Despisistan*.

c.

One might think that the problem lies not really in having objectionable objections but in too overtly expressing them. One of the crucial features of *Enlightened Despisistan* seems to be that the objections, whether they are objectively ill- or well-founded and were reached in either a responsible or irresponsible fashion, are voiced in such a hostile way. As we saw in the passage quoted earlier, Mill demands that the avoidance of the other's society should not be "parade[d]." Perhaps *Enlightened Despisistan* would look much more hospitable if there were clear moral norms of how to express one's objections or under which circumstances one should not express them at all.

One has to remember that one can express even valid objections in a morally problematic way. Take, for instance, two situations in which a valid objection is publicly uttered. First, it could be voiced in a civilized and friendly discussion that despite all disagreements conveys equal respect and even esteem for the further opinions of the other. Second, it could be expressed in a way that undermines or aims at undermining the social status and/or the self-conception of the other person, either as an equal citizen demanding respect or as someone whose particular identity is something to be esteemed. To show that an objection is expressed in a disrespectful way, one will have to refer to certain minimal standards of comportment that are universally valid, even for criticizing a criminal for her deeds. Criticizing the expression of a valid objection as lacking in esteem will, in contrast, have to highlight the fact that an objection might paint a distorting image of the criticized worldview or practice if it does not take account of those features that are valuable despite the objection. Thus the crucial question to ask is, What forms of expressing objections are ruled out by the respect conception?

All these three dimensions have to be considered in order to determine what kind of objections are objectionable. Whereas the first rules out some objections as to be overcome immediately, the second alerts us to the care we have to invest in forming such potentially hurtful objections. Although there are additional norms governing the expression of objections, the fundamental problem of having certain objections in the first place imposes a duty on us to reconsider how we form them. As this duty becomes more salient, the more these objections will likely be expressed in a hurtful manner.

5. THE IMPERFECT DUTY OF ESTEEM LEARNING

In what follows, I argue that the objection component has to be guided by an imperfect duty to, first, try to change one's ethical objection from strongly felt condemnation to mere disagreement and perhaps even to either indifference or affirmation and, second, if that is not possible, to acknowledge other values that might soften the initial objection. This move brings the respect conception much closer to any reasonable version of the esteem conception.

It is important to distinguish two interpretations of an esteem conception, which can be embraced either *instead of* or *in addition to* the respect conception. The first reading, which Forst opposes, *grounds* toleration in esteem.[31] Such toleration can be witnessed, for instance, between friends and family members who tolerate the other's bad habits only because they love or esteem them. The second interpretation is much weaker. It is a respect conception that argues that we should esteem others as much as possible. Toleration, correctly understood, then demands of us to try to overcome it, even if that will not always be possible. I believe that this best captures what Forst's respect conception ought to demand in light of potentially harmful objections.

Outside of the context of toleration, something along these lines has been proposed by Charles Taylor. Acknowledging that there can be no right to be equally esteemed as that would undermine the very process of authentic evaluation, he asks us to approach other cultures with a presumption that they will contain something valuable if they "animated whole societies over a considerable stretch of time."[32] He refers to Hans-Georg Gadamer's "fusion of horizons,"[33] which makes it necessary to transcend one's own framework in order to adequately appreciate the other's standpoint. Interestingly, Taylor believes that the main reason people withhold this presumption and the required engagement is "a mixture of prejudice and ill-will,"[34] which he interprets as a lack of respect.

However, as an imperfect duty, another reason is available. Such a fusion of horizons is very time-consuming and cannot be applied to all cultures and diverging viewpoints one encounters in a multicultural society. Thus some neglect might be justifiable. However, not engaging in such an endeavor will be more problematic if we are dealing not only with a lack of positive esteem but with a statement of negative value, perhaps even condemnation. And this imperfect duty will be more urgent the more the condemnation is forcefully expressed by the majority, as in *Enlightened Despisistan*. We might also follow Barbara Herman in explaining how we ought to be responsive to the vulnerability of agents and their agency to our actions:[35] to the extent the minority indeed "needs" not to be despised, it is imperative for the majority to at least attempt to overcome its negative attitudes, even if, in the last instance, it ends up not being able to embrace indifference or even affirmation.

In the same vein, Axel Honneth has spoken of a right of cultural minorities "in a weak sense [. . .] to be judged according to an 'anticipation of completeness' (Gadamer) of their value."[36] The notion of a "weak" right is misleading insofar as we are dealing with an imperfect duty. However, insisting on some kind of right highlights that a claim is involved here and that disregarding it might in extreme cases amount to a moral wrong.

This duty is stronger if one is a member of a majority culture. And if we do not do so, we have to give moral reasons why we are permitted not even to try (or not try so hard). This thought explains the intuition that there is something problematic about mere toleration if it does not involve at least an attempt at more. Note that this imperfect duty to try to esteem the other as much as possible is, I believe, not reciprocally and generally rejectable. It is thus an understatement if Forst argues that beyond mere prejudices overcoming one's objections "can amount to nothing more than an ethical-political ideal."[37] The imperfect duty I highlight also plays an important role in the political context and may be subsumed under the "readiness to accept discursive responsibility in normative conflicts."[38] Discursive responsibility here applies not only to presenting one's own reasons but to listening to those of others. This is the very idea of the discourse's ethical emphasis on mutual role taking. However, given different contexts, it might be important to distinguish different forms of role taking. For the political and legal sphere, it is probably enough to see that one has to accept the other's view as reasonable. This contains some amount of esteem for the cohesiveness of the other's argumentation but not necessarily for its content. Yet when Forst argues that not all objections can be overcome when they are "cases of persistent mutual objections,"[39] I take it that the qualifier "persistent mutual" is supposed to indicate that enough discussion from both sides has taken place so that both parties to the conflict know about the values involved for the other. In that case, the imperfect duty of esteem learning might have been fulfilled if the discussion was guided by an explicit acknowledgment of that duty.

Especially within the cultural sphere, it seems important to not only constrain the legal and political application of one's ethical views but remain aware that they are merely ethical and that their formation as well as expression should be constrained by the imperfect moral duty of esteem learning. As argued previously, I believe that the demand for a well-founded ethical objection already entails this by it being well-founded with regard to the basis of the objection *as well as* with regard to the object of the objection. This becomes obvious where Forst asks those critical of the hijab to adequately appreciate the complex meanings that are given to it by the women who wear the hijab.[40] And although I agree with Forst that neither in this case nor in that of homosexual struggles for equal (marriage) rights should the right be grounded in esteem, esteem still plays a vital role. For instance, in the latter case, a crucial lack of reciprocity lies in not adequately applying certain standards that are supposed to explain the value of heterosexual relationships (loyalty, stability, and authenticity of love) to homosexual relationships in which they are manifest as well. Any legal privileging of certain aspects (be it of being married or of raising children) must indicate why such privileging is justified. Here Forst seems to agree when he writes that justice demands to treat homosexual and heterosexual couples on an equal footing, "not just in a positive-legal but also in a symbolic sense."[41]

At least in some cases, the respect conception, properly understood, thus entails a move toward the weak version of the esteem conception. *Enlightened Despisistan* is not only a hostile but also an unjust society because, given the breadth of the objections held by the majority, one cannot but assume that the members of the majority must unjustly fail to see what is valuable in the minority cultures, even if only presupposing their own partial standards. And this evaluative blindness will at least partly also explain the intensity of the contempt. In addition, *Enlightened Despisistan* falls short on the crucial though imperfect duty of esteem learning. And finally, its majority members seem to lack the

73

moral decency to express their objections in ways that convey respect and due esteem. Although the realm of objectionable objections still has to be analyzed further, it seems to be much broader than it might have initially appeared.

74

NOTES

1. Rainer Forst, "Toleration and Its Paradoxes: A Tribute to John Horton," *Philosophia* 45 (2017): 415–24, here 416.
2. Rainer Forst, *Toleration in Conflict: Past and Present* (Cambridge: Cambridge University Press, 2013), 18.
3. Ibid., 489–90; Rainer Forst, *The Right to Justification: Elements of a Constructivist Theory of Justice* (New York: Columbia University Press, 2012), 20–21.
4. Forst, "Toleration and Its Paradoxes," 418.
5. Forst, *Toleration in Conflict,* 505.
6. Ibid., 31–32.
7. Forst, *Right to Justification,* 150. Forst also discusses a fourth conception, the "coexistence" conception, in which two roughly equally powerful groups tolerate each other in a modus vivendi—that is, out of fear of an open conflict in itself or of the other side prevailing in it.
8. I borrow the term *esteem learning* from Frank Nullmeier, *Politische Theorie des Sozialstaats* (Frankfurt am Main: Campus, 2000), 406.
9. In a pluralistic society consisting of many small communities without a clear majority, the problem might not be as urgent. However, it is likely that if there is something amiss with the society as I am describing it here, something is also amiss with smaller communities ethically despising many or even all traits of each other.
10. *Enlightened Despisistan* is thus crucially different from a merely indifferent society where nobody in the wider society esteems any specific traits of yours, with the exception of your fellow members of the minority group.
11. Forst, *Toleration in Conflict,* 519.
12. Ibid.
13. Ibid.
14. Ibid., 505.
15. Ibid., 512.
16. Ibid., 514.
17. John Stuart Mill, "On Liberty," in *On Liberty and Other Essays,* ed. John Gray (Oxford: Oxford University Press, 1991), 1–128, here 85–86.
18. Rainer Forst, *Justification and Critique: Towards a Critical Theory of Politics* (Cambridge: Polity, 2014), 133.
19. See for an elaboration of this concept Will Kymlicka, *Multicultural Citizenship: A Liberal Theory of Minority Rights* (Oxford: Oxford University Press, 1996), chap. 5.

20. Axel Honneth, *Freedom's Right: The Social Foundations of Democratic Life* (New York: Columbia University Press, 2014).

21. Forst is aware that the distinction between ethics and morality does not coincide with whether the criteria of reciprocity and generality lead to nonrejectability. As the latter distinction is the crucial one that can only be procedurally established, even objections that have as its content issues of justice and morality fall under the category of reasonable disagreements. See *Right to Justification,* 64, 68.

22. Forst, *Toleration in Conflict,* 19.

23. John Horton, "Toleration as Virtue," in *Toleration: An Elusive Virtue,* ed. David Heyd (Princeton: Princeton University Press, 1996), 28–43, here 38.

24. Forst, *Toleration in Conflict,* 19.

25. Forst, "Toleration and Its Paradoxes," 510.

26. Forst, *Toleration in Conflict,* 20 (italics added).

27. Ibid., 19.

28. Ibid., 20.

29. For the distinction between intrinsic and extrinsic racism, see Kwame Anthony Appiah, "Racisms," in *The Anatomy of Racism,* ed. David T. Goldberg (Minneapolis: University of Minnesota Press, 1990), 3–17.

30. Descriptively, most tolerant racists may merely be tolerant on the basis of the three other conceptions of toleration: they may fear the opposing group or a third party's retaliation without a tolerant modus vivendi (coexistence conception), they may make a rather arbitrary exception to the individual's deepest beliefs (permission conception), or they may esteem certain features of the other's life-style, although the person herself is regarded as not having a right (a certain variation of the esteem conception that grounds toleration in esteem and *not* respect). However, although these descriptions might better fit most actual racists who happen to be tolerant, they are not conceptually necessary.

31. Appiah, "Racisms," 31–32.

32. Charles Taylor, "The Politics of Recognition," in *Multiculturalism: Examining the Politics of Recognition,* ed. Amy Gutmann (Princeton: Princeton University Press, 1994), 25–73, here 66.

33. Ibid., 67.

34. Ibid., 67–68.

35. Barbara Herman, "The Scope of Moral Requirement," *Philosophy & Public Affairs* 30, no. 3 (2001): 227–56.

36. Axel Honneth, "Redistribution as Recognition: A Response to Nancy Fraser," in *Redistribution or Recognition? A Political-Philosophical Exchange,* by Nancy Fraser and Axel Honneth (New York: Verso, 2003), 110–97, here 168–69.

37. Forst, *Toleration in Conflict,* 536.

38. Ibid., 504.

39. Ibid., 536.

40. Ibid., 557.

41. Ibid., 566.

CHAPTER 5

The Right to Justification and the Good of Nonalienation

Catherine Lu

1. INTRODUCTION

Rainer Forst's critical theory of justice is based on a powerful principle of autonomy. This Kantian-inspired theory understands all human beings to have a "claim to be respected as an autonomous subject of justification; that is, to be respected in one's dignity as a being who can provide and demand justifications and who should have the status of a free and equal normative authority within a normative order of binding rules and institutions."[1]

As participants in social relations, individuals have a basic human right to the justification of the political and social structures that mediate their moral and political agency, organize their activities and interactions, and produce their social positions and conditions. Viewed against a historical backdrop of despotic, authoritarian, and colonial rule, it is surely a potent principle of justice that asserts that those who are subjected to the basic structure "should be the subjects, and not merely the objects, of justification."[2] Because the right to justification is universal, justice "demands that every political and social basic structure must be justified to all those subject to it with arguments that cannot be reciprocally and generally rejected."[3] Forst has developed the right to justification primarily as a principle of fundamental justice that serves the emancipatory aim of disestablishing domination, or arbitrary social and political power.

I am interested in the potential of Forst's theory of justice for guiding a progressive transformation of contemporary structural injustices associated with historical colonialism that continue to be reproduced in domestic, international, and transnational orders. I argue that Forst's focus on the intrinsic relationship between a rightful social/political order and the moral autonomy of agents is an important aid in diagnosing what exactly is wrong with contemporary social relations at various levels that suffer from colonial histories and unsurpassed structural injustices stemming from those histories. In terms of guiding the reform of extant institutions or social practices, however, Forst could be more explicit about how to structure the relationship between actually existing orders or practices of justification or how to resolve conflicts among them. For example, if we consider the international human rights doctrine to be a contemporary instantiation of a universalized right to justification, does Forst's theory justify or disapprove of international or external actors overriding the collective self-determination of some already marginalized or disadvantaged groups whose social practices may come into conflict with such standards?

Forst might respond by arguing that claims to group self-determination cannot license the violation of the moral rights of some vulnerable category of persons within the group. The basic human right to justification is inalienable, and it is the role of a critical theory of justice to call into question all existing social forms and explicitly challenge the legitimacy of any basic structure predicated on denying or obscuring such a right to any portion of its members. While I agree with Forst that all existing social forms and practices can be subject to critique in principle, colonial hierarchies of domination in world history have taken the forms of external agents usurping collective self-determination, disrupting and colonizing socialization processes, and destroying the conditions and structures of self-governance. Given this history, for Forst's account of the right to justification to serve emancipatory ends, it needs an account of how practices and structures of justification should be related to each other. Both morally and practically, a critical and emancipatory theory of justice should enable progress toward greater justice as an empirically autonomous achievement of those subjected to a social practice—and not only from the standpoint of an ideal standard of moral autonomy.

The risk of neglecting the empirical decisional agency of agents in struggles for justice is that practices of justice and justification may become alienating to those subjected to them. Forst has recently elaborated on the concept of alienation, noting that since the moral status of being a justificatory agent is inalienable, alienation constitutes a problem of justice only if it involves a denial or loss of moral autonomy. While I agree with Forst that what he calls first-order and second-order noumenal alienation are symptomatic of structural injustice, he is too quick to dismiss the normative significance of what I have termed *existential alienation,* which is the loss of an agent's appropriative powers precipitated by the collapse of social frames of meaning that structure the agent's conceptions and pursuit of authentic and meaningful forms of flourishing. This form of alienation, which I base on the concept of alienation developed by Rahel Jaeggi, arises in contexts where a group's socialization processes have been radically disrupted, severed, or discontinued, such as in the case of the economic, political, and cultural destruction experienced by indigenous peoples as well as many other subjugated groups.

Forst draws a sharp distinction between noumenal alienation, which signifies an agent's estranged moral autonomy, and ethical alienation, which signifies an agent's inhibited subjective freedom to pursue certain ethical visions of the good or happy life. I argue, however, that some approximation of ethical nonalienation is a precondition of the possibility of achieving moral autonomy: people cannot fully or adequately develop or exercise their moral autonomy and thus avoid noumenal alienation unless they are also able to avoid existential alienation to a sufficient degree. I use the case of indigenous alienation under settler colonialism to highlight the moral importance of transforming agents' subjectivity in terms of their appropriative agency to realize decolonized notions of the good or ethical life as a prerequisite for motivating and conditioning their nonalienated participation in overcoming noumenal forms of alienation and becoming autonomous agents. My argument here is not communitarian, which criticizes all attempts to "articulate morality in the strong universalist and categorical sense" as "in fact, thick, particular, ethical values and substantive conceptions of the good in disguise."[4] Rather, I am arguing that the good of nonalienated human flourishing is deeply connected to the political project of overcoming forms of noumenal alienation that attend structures and practices of domination. A theory of justice that aims to provide critical resources to contemporary agents for overturning conditions of settler-colonial and postcolonial domination needs to be more sensitive to the deep connection between the right to justification and the good of nonalienation.

2. AUTONOMY AND THE RIGHT TO SELF-DETERMINATION

It is a virtue of Forst's theory of justice that it focuses not only or primarily on the distribution of goods but also on the production of goods. Justice is an "*autonomous* achievement" of political agents and not an independently determined condition of equality in the distribution of goods among passive recipients.[5] According to Forst, "fundamental justice" requires a basic structure of justification "in which social status and social and political power of citizens are equal to the extent that discursive justice can be set in motion as an autonomous political enterprise."[6] What makes the exercise of democratic power just is that it is "exercised through the rule of reciprocally and generally justifiable reasons when it comes to basic questions of justice."[7] The local and domestic are important sites of the right to justification, which must be "exercised, interpreted, and institutionalized in light of the particular self-understanding of the members of the political community, *so that the 'construction' of a basic structure deserves to be called their joint undertaking.*"[8] Practices of justification are not hypothetical: "Ultimately only those affected can themselves carry out the justification of their own basic social structures. This is how critical theory links up with the claims and demands made by social actors themselves in concrete social contexts."[9]

This account of justice that affirms agents as coauthors of the social/political orders to which they are subjected becomes complicated by the recognition that the question of who is "affected" or "subjected" by any social practice is open—"the right to justification does not end at the boundaries of contexts of justification within states."[10] Indeed, Forst acknowledges that in contemporary contexts, local, national, international, and global orders are interconnected in circumstances of politics that are characterized by "multiple domination": "Most often, [the dominated] are dominated by their own (hardly legitimate) governments, elites, or warlords, who in turn are both working together and (at least partly) dominated by global actors. Women and children, in particular, are the subjects of even further relations of domination within the family and local community. . . . The various contexts of justice—local, national, international, and global—are connected through the kind of injustice they produce, and a theory of justice must not remain blind to this interconnectedness."[11] Forst thus argues that a "domestic project of justice cannot be conceived of without a conception of transnational justice."[12] The right to justification beyond borders is important for ensuring that members of a political community do not achieve internal justice at the expense of doing injustice to outsiders as well as for ensuring that external or international regimes do not perpetuate external and/or internal domination.

It is refreshing that in his account of transnational justice, Forst acknowledges the internal complexity of states and the claims of parties below the state level to take part in processes of justification between states or at the transnational level. His account leaves room for transnational politics as a site of contestation to overcome structural injustices that may exist within state borders as well as transcend them. The power of Forst's theory of justification is that no level of social structures, from local to transnational, is immune from justificatory critique: the universality of the right to justification allows for the interrogation of all existing social/political structures for their inadequacies and blind spots with respect to dominated, oppressed, exploited, and marginalized social groups. Such an acknowledgment of the transnational context of injustice and the need to examine critically actually existing social practices, including practices of justification, at all levels is potentially emancipatory in radical ways.

Consider the relationship between the right to justification and the right to political self-determination. The ideal of autonomy underlying the right to justification also translates into a moral right to self-determination, which can serve as a critical standard by which to assess the moral quality of actual social structures. Forst's theory could thus be marshaled to criticize the historical subjugation of peoples in a colonial international order, which involved the usurpation or destruction of the conditions and structures of self-determination among the colonized—and in ways that led to flagrant violations of autonomy that were instantiated in acts and practices of brutal repression, enslavement, exploitation, marginalization, and sometimes outright destruction. Forst's theory could also support criticisms of the contemporary international order, as well as of settler-colonial states, for continuing to deny conditions and structures of self-determination to indigenous peoples. This is particularly important in the recognition of the historical context of settler-colonial practices that were predicated on nineteenth- and early twentieth-century racial ideologies that forecast the inevitable extinction of all indigenous peoples in the course of progress toward civilization. Forst's theory allows us to understand that the ideal of justice as an autonomous achievement is not guaranteed merely by letting already socially recognized agents—in this case, states—participate in existing interstate practices of justification, since, marred as states are by constitutive structural injustices, such practices of "justification might just reproduce these structures of domination."[13] Forst's theory thus could explain the normative significance of the 2007 United Nations Declaration on the Rights of Indigenous Peoples, which asserts the right to self-determination of indigenous peoples, as a progressive continuation of the decolonization process.

At the same time, Forst notes that the right to justification enables members within any social group to contest social structures that may deny or infringe on their rights to justification. Forst's theory thus also can ground international human rights doctrine and various practices of international or external monitoring, assistance, and accountability regarding human rights compliance in the international arena. If we consider international human rights doctrine to be a historical instantiation of a universalized right to justification, however, how does Forst's

82

theory reconcile international mechanisms of justificatory critique with the right to collective self-determination of some marginalized and disadvantaged groups whose social practices may conflict with such standards? Does a universal right to justification necessarily mean that anyone can engage in a justificatory critique of a social practice whether or not they are participants in a particular social or political context? In cases of conflict, whose claim to self-determination ought to prevail?

In a related debate, Forst has been critical of those who argue that critique must always be immanent to a social practice. He asks, somewhat rhetorically, "Who would want to suggest to a critic of the Indian caste system who rejects this system in toto that she should please proceed in an 'immanent' way?"[14] The distinction between "internal," or "immanent," critique and "external," or "transcendental," critique is an artificial opposition: social critique must be sensitive to demands for reciprocity and generality, "even where this is 'unheard of' and goes far beyond the firmly established understandings of justifiability or ethical life. . . . Settled ethical life is the *object* of criticism, not its *ground* or *limit*. Critical theory cannot dispense with the transcending power of reason, which may venture into regions that were previously unthinkable."[15] It is important to note that Forst does not equate immanent critique with "insider" critique and transcendent critique with "outsider" critique. According to Forst, individual agents, while socially situated, are also autonomous, leading to a blurring of immanent and transcendent practice: "Nobody is entirely absorbed into the practice of justification in which he or she participates, because it is always possible to subject the practice to reflexive questioning and criticism."[16] The hard question, however, is whether a universal right to justification translates automatically into an overriding or transcendental right— possessed not only by agents within a particular social context but also by those who are external to it—to justify criticism and perhaps even other forms of intervention to change the social practice when fortified by the transcending power of reason.

It is not clear, then, how a right to justification would not override the empirical exercise of decisional autonomy by members of a political community to maintain their own basic structure as *their* joint undertaking—when such a structure may be morally defective in meeting *internal* justice demands—compared to an external model. The danger is that the right to justification may then justify usurpation or coercive interference in political communities if the external (national or international) regime asserts an objectively more justi-   83 fied standard of justice than the internal model. In such a scenario, there could be a conflict of rights to justification between members within a particular community as well as between some members of that community and the external community, and it is not clear how asserting a universal right to justification alone can resolve the conflict. Such scenarios have arisen in various forms. In Canada, for example, a version of this conflict appears in debates about whether the Canadian Charter of Rights and Freedoms ought to be applicable by judicial decree to indigenous peoples whose inherent right to self-determination is recognized in Canadian constitutional law.[17] In that case, as well as in many other contexts, issues such as gender equality and democratic rights that are unequivocally part of international human rights doctrine remain contested principles and practices in many social structures.[18]

The right to justification, when universalized, may thus challenge or undermine rather than affirm the right to group self-determination, even of those groups that have historically suffered denials of group self-determination in colonial contexts. Forst might argue that the democratization of practices of justification is a basic minimum for any social order to be plausibly regarded as a "joint undertaking," but the validity of democracy promotion by external powerful states and the international community is deeply disputed: "The imperative of democratization, both at the domestic and multilateral levels, is construed by some as a liberal and cosmopolitan ideal, as a form of neo-colonialism, as historical progress, or as an effect of Western-led globalization."[19] While some of the reasons underlying critical assessments may reflect the (unreasonable) complaints of intransigent domestic elites, it is plausible that given the structural legacies of colonial injustice on the development of international order, there is also reasonable criticism and disagreement about the emancipatory potential of an internationalized democratization agenda.

It matters a great deal, then, how various levels and structures of justification ought to be related in international and transnational contexts. Forst clearly asserts that international structures should not themselves be dominating or assist in perpetuating internal domination within groups, but his theory may benefit from a more explicit account of how the right to justification would discipline the use of coercive intervention by international or external agents to assist internal members of a problematic social structure to transform those problematic structures. What normative guidance does the right to justification give to those seeking to transform an objectionable social practice so that their efforts do not reproduce relations and structures of domination that were the hallmark of a colonial international order? The fundamental question is how essential it is, in Forst's account, that agents *within* a particular social structure struggle for and produce justice *themselves* so that they are collectively responsible for *becoming* morally autonomous agents. If it is essential to achieve progress toward the realization of justice as an autonomous achievement, structures of justification, at both domestic and international levels, must also aim to be nonalienating toward those who are subjected to them. Forst's account of the right to justification thus needs to be supplemented by a certain account of the good of nonalienation.

3. AUTONOMY AND NONALIENATION

Forst ties the basic right to justification to a conception of human dignity, where the violation of such dignity "consists in being ignored, not counting, and being 'invisible' for the purposes of legitimating social relations."[20] Democracy respects human dignity when "understood as a process of criticism and justification, both within and outside of institutions, in which those who are subjected to rule become the co-authors of their political order."[21] In recent work, Forst has expanded on how the denial of such dignity produces morally objectionable forms of alienation. While noting that alienation can be conceptualized in different ways, Forst develops an account of "noumenal alienation" as a "loss of autonomy," which "results from a lack of being recognized or a lack of recognizing yourself as an agent of justification equal to others, as having an equal right to justification. . . . In this sense, alienation violates the *dignity of humans as moral and political law-givers*—a dignity seen by Rousseau, Kant and Marx as *inalienable*: It can be denied or violated, but it cannot be lost."[22] In Forst's account, then, a social/political order is justified when based on principles whose justifications cannot be generally and reciprocally rejected, and the establishment of such an order cannot be alienating to those subjected to it in a morally objectionable sense, since it is alienation from one's equal status as a justificatory agent that must be overcome, from a moral point of view.

Forst distinguishes between first-order and second-order noumenal alienation: a denial of one's standing by others as "a rational normative authority equal to all others" constitutes first-order noumenal alienation, whereas the self-denial of a subject, who does not consider herself or himself an equal normative authority—or an "end in oneself"—constitutes second-order noumenal alienation. The account of second-order noumenal alienation partly acknowledges that agents who are dominated sometimes may lack the self-respect required to engage in the struggle against first-order noumenal alienation, or the denial of equal moral and political status by others. As Forst puts it, "To struggle for such a status presupposes a form of self-respect that is lost in second order noumenal alienation. Therefore the first task is to attack and overcome second order noumenal alienation—by radical critique, the public use of reason, and sober social analysis. The 'mysticism' of the dominating and alienating normative order must be dispelled and the sense of one's own worth as a justificatory agent equal to others must be appealed to and furthered."[23] Forst's account of second-order noumenal self-alienation shares resemblances with descriptions of one of the most damaging aspects of colonialism. Frantz Fanon has written extensively on the cultural and psychological harms inflicted by colonial relationships: the colonized are "people in whom an inferiority complex has taken root, whose local cultural originality has been committed to the grave" and who must "position themselves in relation to the civilizing language: i.e., the metropolitan culture."[24] How can such internalized forms of oppression be overcome? This is an important task, since in Forst's theory, valid principles of justice are those that could be held "in a reciprocal and general manner if those subject to the norms were their free and equal authors. *That they should become*

such authors is the first requirement of justice."[25] While Forst's call for
the demystification of social structures of hierarchical domination has
Marxist roots, it is unclear in Forst's account whether the strategies he
proposes of "radical critique, the public use of reason, and sober social
analysis"[26] are meant as recommendations to the oppressed. One difficulty is that those who are thoroughly self-alienated may be the least
well-equipped to engage in the effective use of these strategies: they are
unlikely to have the requisite self-respect required to mount a radical
critique or to participate effectively in the space of public reason distorted by structural injustice; nor is their public engagement likely to
conform to the standards of sober social analysis.

With respect to colonial legacies, the challenge of agents *becoming*
free and equal authors of their social structures is not resolved by others
conferring on them the status of persons as justificatory equals or even
in the agents themselves developing a view of themselves as "justificatory equals who determine themselves individually and collectively as
autonomous normative authorities."[27] As Glen Coulthard has argued,
following Frantz Fanon, dominated agents need to struggle to create
new decolonized terms of justification that they can call their own and
not only seek equal justificatory status based on structures of colonial
power, otherwise "the colonized will have failed to reestablish themselves as truly self-determining: as creators of the terms, values, and
conditions by which they are to be recognized."[28]

To understand the distinct additional challenge, I draw on the work
of Rahel Jaeggi, who has developed a conception of alienation that
refers to experiences of disconnection, disruption, or distortion in
"the structure of human relations to self and world" and "the relations
agents have to themselves, to their own actions, and to the social and
natural worlds." Jaeggi conceives of alienation as a "particular form
of the loss of freedom" that involves "a relation of disturbed or inhibited appropriation of world and self." Successful appropriation by an
agent "can be explicated as the capacity to make the life one leads, or
what one wills and does, one's own; as the capacity to identify with
oneself and with what one does; in other words, as the ability to realize oneself in what one does."[29] This activity of self-realization in the
world is typically disrupted or distorted in individuals and societies

that have experienced colonial injustice. Pratap Mehta, for example, has observed that an empire creates "a new existential order," in which the subordinated face a dilemma: "To assert a difference from the normative hierarchies that imperial powers created was to confirm the very thing the colonizer thought about you. But to assimilate to those demands and fashion yourself in accordance with them was to grant him the ultimate victory. The estrangement that colonialism produced was not so much a substantive estrangement—Am I estranged from my tradition?—but an almost existential one. *Nothing the colonial subject did could be seen to be authentically his own.*"[30] Jonathan Lear also captures this form of *existential* alienation in the experience of indigenous peoples whose particular social and moral frames have been disrupted, even rendered inoperable or unintelligible, through colonial settlement, exploitation, genocide, and dispossession.[31] Lear recounts how the last great chief of the Crow nation, Plenty Coups, described his people's eventual confinement to a reserve: "When the buffalo went away the hearts of my people fell to the ground, and they could not lift them up again. After this nothing happened."[32] Lear interprets this statement to reveal the very loss of normative concepts with which to construct any meaningful narrative about being a Crow in the world. Crucially, this loss goes beyond being denied the "power to tell the story, or conflicting narratives."[33]

Existential alienation is distinct from the noumenal forms developed by Forst. In the case of first-order noumenal alienation, dominated agents are deprived of the status of being justificatory equals by others, but it is assumed that being a justificatory agent in the particular social order is consistent with how agents identify with or realize themselves in the world. In Forst's account of second-order noumenal alienation, dominated agents do not see themselves as justificatory equals, but the reason is that they have internalized their inferior status and naturalized the social order that denies them such standing. In conditions of settler colonialism, however, indigenous agents may be not only alienated from their status as justificatory equals but also alienated from a social, ethical, normative, and material order that is predicated on denying the very possibility of realizing indigenous ways of being—knowledge, philosophy, governance, or culture—in conditions of modernity. The alienation that stems from a loss of agents' appropriative powers may have effects on their capacity to assert their standing as justificatory equals and hence inhibit their moral autonomy, but its primary effect is to render agents incapable of flourishing in authentic and meaningful ways in the social world, which thus inhibits their subjective freedom, understood as self-realization.[34] As Jaeggi has observed, this form of alienation "is not coextensive with heteronomy" and depends on more than whether agents enjoy self-determination in the negative sense of not being subject to a foreign will.[35]

Forst has noted that his "non-ethical understanding of the condition of alienation to be overcome" contrasts with Rahel Jaeggi's conception of alienation, which refers primarily to an "ethical problem."[36] He also asserts that whereas there is a categorical imperative to overcome noumenal alienation by dismantling domination, "certain ideals of self-realization or social life that do not rest on such moral foundations may still be well-founded but cannot claim the same kind of validity. They appeal to the attractiveness of the ethical vision they express but they ground no strong moral duties."[37] In cases where domination has produced not only noumenal forms of alienation but also existential alienation, however, the transformation of social structures toward justice must surely require establishing conditions of possibility for agents to overcome existential alienation and recover their subjective freedom as appropriative agents who can meaningfully engage in activities of self-realization. Such a task entails a stronger connection between ethical and moral forms of autonomy.[38]

The struggle against second-order noumenal alienation involves dismantling the burdensome veil of dominating structures and practices that either makes dominated agents incapable of seeing the insult paid to their self-respect or damages their self-respect to the point of producing acquiescence to domination. A significant source of damage to the social bases of self-respect for indigenous peoples in settler-colonial states lies in the destruction of indigenous forms of life, including languages, cultures, and governance structures. Overcoming existential alienation requires more and different tasks than dismantling structures of settler-colonial domination that continue to constitute domestic political orders, such as Canada, as well as international order.

As Leanne Simpson, an indigenous writer and educator, has put it, "We [Indigenous peoples] need to be able to articulate in a clear manner our visions for the future, for living as Indigenous Peoples in contemporary times. . . . [This involves] articulating and living our legal systems; language learning; ceremonial and spiritual pursuits; creating and using our artistic and performance-based traditions."[39] Overcoming existential alienation thus involves strategies of self-affirmation and self-development[40] at the same time that it may require state and international support for the revival of indigenous languages, cultures, and governance, since their resurgence is a precondition for indigenous peoples being able to engage in decolonized struggles to become free and equal authors of the social world. While existential alienation points to an ethical challenge in postcolonial conditions, it is also a deeply moral challenge, because without overcoming existential alienation, agents cannot develop or exercise meaningful moral autonomy. In this way, the good of nonalienation in an ethical sense is a precondition for moral autonomy.

4. CONCLUSION

Rainer Forst, in a rich body of work, has articulated a "radical conception of justice" that centrally interrogates the *"first question of justice*—the justifiability of social relations and the distribution of the 'power of justification' within a political context."[41] Critical theory takes history and contexts of power relations into account in thinking about how to conceptualize political struggles for justice as emancipatory projects of agents developing their moral autonomy. This means that critical theory acknowledges that the starting point of all theorizing is some context—or multiple contexts—of structural injustice or domination, to which theorizing about justice aims to respond. Forst's critical theory of justice aims to empower socially situated agents to diagnose and criticize existing power relations in their social relations, with a view to illuminating avenues of emancipatory politics in multiple contexts of domination. I have argued that Forst's powerful account of the right to justification, grounded in a Kantian notion of moral autonomy, can help us make sense of colonialism as a historical wrong, as well as diagnose the reproduction of colonial power structures in contemporary international and transnational relations.

90   At the same time, I have been concerned to analyze the constructive potential of Forst's theory for guiding anticolonial struggle in contemporary contexts. For a critical theory of justice, such as Forst's, to be socially grounded, it is important that it be nonalienating. This is an especially important consideration in contexts of transnational and indigenous-settler colonial relations. The good of nonalienation is an ethical claim, not a claim of justice, but it constitutes a regulative ideal that supports the progression toward greater justice. Part of the justification for struggles for justice to be engaged "from within a political and social context of struggles for a better society, a context of mutual obligations and of solidarities,"[42] is that ethical nonalienation is a precondition for agents developing and exercising their moral autonomy in meaningful ways. The conception of justice as an autonomous achievement of political agents presupposes the successful resolution of the problem of existential alienation, otherwise structures of justification, even when reformed to grant standing to agents as justificatory equals, may nevertheless continue to be sources of intersubjective domination.

NOTES

The author wishes to thank Pablo Gilabert, Amy Allen, and Eduardo Mendieta for their constructive comments.

1. Rainer Forst, *Normativity and Power: Analyzing Social Orders of Justification* (Oxford: Oxford University Press, 2017), 202.
2. Rainer Forst, *Justification and Critique,* trans. Ciaran Cronin (Malden, MA: Polity, 2014), 3.
3. Rainer Forst, *The Right to Justification* (New York: Columbia University Press, 2012), 249.
4. Amy Allen, *The End of Progress: Decolonizing the Normative Foundations of Critical Theory* (New York: Columbia University Press, 2015), 145.
5. Rainer Forst, *Justice, Democracy and the Right to Justification* (New York: Bloomsbury, 2014), 212.
6. Ibid., 211.
7. Forst, *Normativity and Power,* 70.
8. Forst, *Right to Justification,* 262 (italics added).

9. Ibid., 259 and 262.

10. Forst, *Normativity and Power*, 8.

11. Forst, *Right to Justification*, 257.

12. Ibid., 263.

13. Rainer Forst, "A Critical Theory of Politics: Grounds, Method, and Aims," *Philosophy & Social Criticism* 41, no. 3 (2015): 225–34 at 230.

14. Forst, *Normativity and Power*, 13.

15. Ibid.

16. Forst, *Justification and Critique*, 4.

17. See Aki-Kwe and Mary Ellen Turpel, "Aboriginal Peoples and the Canadian Charter of Rights and Freedoms," *Canadian Woman Studies* 10, nos. 2–3 (1989): 149–57; and Kent McNeil, "Aboriginal Governments and the Canadian Charter of Rights and Freedoms," *Osgoode Hall Law Journal* 34, no. 1 (1996): 61–99.

18. On gender justice, see Sally Engle Merry, *Human Rights and Gender Violence: Translating International Law into Local Justice* (Chicago: University of Chicago Press, 2006).

19. Vincent Pouliot and Jean-Philippe Thérien, "Global Governance: A Struggle over Universal Values," *International Studies Review* 20, no. 1 (2018): 55–73, at 69.

20. Forst, *Justification and Critique*, 98.

21. Forst, *Normativity and Power*, 20.

22. Rainer Forst, "Noumenal Alienation: Rousseau, Kant and Marx on the Dialectics of Self-Determination," in *Kantian Review* 24, no. 4 (2017): 523–51, at 523.

23. Forst, "Noumenal Alienation," 544.

24. Frantz Fanon, *Black Skin, White Masks*, trans. Richard Philcox (1952; repr., New York: Grove, 2008), 2.

25. Forst, *Justification and Critique*, 5 (italics added).

26. Forst, "Noumenal Alienation," 544.

27. Ibid., 530.

28. Glen Sean Coulthard, *Red Skin, White Masks: Rejecting the Colonial Politics of Recognition* (Minneapolis: University of Minnesota Press, 2014), 39.

29. Rahel Jaeggi, *Alienation*, trans. F. Neuhouse and A. E. Smith (New York: Columbia University Press, 2014), xxi, 2, 22, 36, and 37.

30. Pratap Bhanu Mehta, "After Colonialism: The Impossibility of Self-Determination," in *Colonialism and Its Legacies*, ed. Jacob T. Levy and Iris Marion Young (Lanham, MD: Lexington Books, 2011), 147–70 at 150 and 151.

31. I develop more fully elsewhere the challenge of existential alienation as well as its implications for overcoming interactional and structural forms of alienation in conditions of settler colonialism. See my *Justice and Reconciliation in World Politics* (Cambridge: Cambridge University Press, 2017), 182–216.

32. Jonathan Lear, *Radical Hope: Ethics in the Face of Cultural Devastation* (Cambridge: Harvard University Press, 2006), 50.

33. Ibid.

34. It should be noted that it is the capacity of agents to integrate and appropriate the social conditions they inhabit that is important for authentic flourishing rather than a constancy of substantive orientations or identifications. For further elaboration, see my *Justice and Reconciliation*, 204–14.

35. Jaeggi, *Alienation*, 200.

36. In previous work, Forst noted "important parallels" between Jaeggi's underlying concept of autonomy and the political concept of autonomy that he proposes (*Justification and Critique,* 169). In his most recent work, however, Forst asserts, "Moral autonomy is different from ethical authenticity or happiness, and the two notions of non-alienation they refer to are also conceptually different." See his essay "Noumenal Alienation," 535.

37. Forst, "Noumenal Alienation," 547.

38. As Forst has explained, "A person is ethically autonomous when she determines what is important for herself on the basis of reasons that most fully and adequately take her identity into account, as the person she has been, as she is seen, as she wants to be seen, and to see herself in the present and the future"; Forst, *Right to Justification,* 131.

39. See Leanne Simpson, *Dancing on Our Turtle's Back: Stories of Nishnaabeg Re-creation, Resurgence and a New Emergence* (Winnipeg: Arbeiter Ring, 2011), 17.

40. See also Coulthard, *Red Skin, White Masks.*

41. Forst, *Right to Justification,* 4.

42. Ibid., 262.

CHAPTER 6

"A Certain Relation in the Space of Justifications"

Intentions, Lateral Effects, and Rainer Forst's Concept of Noumenal Power

John P. McCormick

This chapter highlights the significant theoretical advantages that Rainer Forst's concept of noumenal power[1] holds over alternative conceptions, especially self-styled "realist" ones. I proceed to highlight certain ambiguities concerning intentionality and the relationship of thought and action in Forst's conception—particularly as these pertain to his argument that actions beyond physical threat, such as acts of persuasion, should count as exercises of noumenal power. Finally, I suggest—drawing on Michel Foucault and Niccolò Machiavelli—that the concept of noumenal power loses some explanatory force when one considers "lateral effects"—that is, when one moves from a two-actor model of political power to a multiactor model. Forst may overstate the extent to which noumenal power, characterized by reason giving, operates in the realm of politics conceived more broadly. More specifically, Forst may underestimate the extent to which non-reason-giving, objectivizing forms of power must invariably and inevitably constitute the political realm: a realm within which noumenal power certainly plays an important role but not the comprehensive role intimated by Forst.

1. POWER AND LEGITIMACY

The exercise of power is fundamental to politics. That some person or persons must induce others into acting in a certain way or prevent them from acting in a particular way is *the* inescapable fact of politics. No less a luminary of critical theory than György Lukács agrees. His aspiration for a postrevolutionary condition when there would be no politics but only ethics implicitly assumes that politics presupposes the potentially unwelcome and perhaps deleterious influence of some persons over others.

The central question for moral and political philosophy, therefore, is not whether power will be exercised in the realm of politics but rather whether it can be exercised *legitimately*. "Legitimately" usually means that some person or persons exercise power over others with the latter's *consent* to do so, or it means that they exercise power in a way that comports with the objective *interests* of the latter. However, since the seventeenth century, political philosophers have employed "consent" and "interests" within conceptions of legitimacy that are either so formal as to be empty (e.g., Thomas Hobbes) or so substantive as to lapse into self-contradiction (e.g., Jean-Jacques Rousseau).

Furthermore, even the most seemingly benign notions of "consent" and "objective interests" can serve as ideological vehicles for domination—that is, for decidedly *illegitimate* exercises of power. Few, if any, contemporary theorists argue this case as perspicaciously and spiritedly as one of our gracious hosts and editors of this volume, Amy Allen.[2]

The "realist tradition" of political theory, typified by Max Weber, capitulates to or even chauvinistically celebrates the darker implications of political power.[3] Power, for Weber, (almost) always entails subordination and domination. Power means compelling other people to behave in a manner that they otherwise wouldn't, forcing them to do things that they otherwise would not have done. Weber and his devotees argue with much bravado that the threat of physical violence is the operative motivating factor in relationships of power, and they imply—and even sometimes insist—that the exercise of power always or preeminently benefits those who wield power rather than those over whom power is wielded.

Rainer Forst's concept of noumenal power accomplishes, among other important things, the following: (1) it exposes the facile and, ironically, rather naïve quality of Weberian notions of power, which bake physical force and subordination into the very definition of power, and (2) it revives a debate over the conditions of possibility for legitimately exercised political power—one that replaces or at least subtly reconfigures the ideas of "consent" and "interest" that have been used in either overly idealistic or self-contradictory ways in the history of moral-political philosophy. Impressively, Forst, on the one hand, effectively refutes Weber, and, on the other, he lays the groundwork for the reconstruction of a notion of legitimacy that transcends the shortcomings of Hobbes's and Rousseau's vaunted efforts.

2. NOUMENAL POWER: MEANS AND ENDS

As Forst argues persuasively, the "realist" reduction of power to relations of subordination and domination renders impossible any effort to conceptualize legitimate forms of the exercise of power.[4] Alternatively, Forst takes a refreshingly agnostic approach to power: its exercise may be *dominating* of those it targets or even perhaps, as it were, *empowering* of them in significant respects. As Forst writes, "I defend a normatively neutral notion of power that enables us to distinguish more particular forms of power, such as rule, coercion, or domination."[5] In order to conceptualize forms of power that might actually enable, rather than exclusively constrain, those over whom power is exercised, Forst directs our attention away from the instruments of physical violence that so captivate realists. Power per se is not primarily or in any simple way reducible to "the 'hard power' of coercion . . . material stuff, like political [offices], monetary means or, ultimately, military instruments of force."[6] Provocatively, but in a way that fits perfectly with his broader philosophical corpus, Forst argues that, on the contrary, "the real and general phenomenon of power is to be found in the noumenal realm, or better . . . in the 'space of reasons,' [a space] understood as the realm of justifications."[7]

Noumenal power is exercised, according to Forst, when actor A provides *reasons* to actor B that motivate the latter to think or act in a way that they might not otherwise have. This conceptual flexibility concerning the thoughts and/or actions of subjects of power will prove somewhat problematic, as I'll suggest later. But for now, at a definitional level, Forst is agnostic as to whether or not the *means* of reason giving by person A are acceptable from a moral standpoint or whether the *change* that they effect in subject B benefits or harms that person. As long as reasons have been provided by A and a directly resulting change has occurred in the thought or action of B, noumenal power has been exercised by A over B.

By redefining power in this way, Forst conceptually expands the range of *means* available for exercising power beyond means that merely entail physical threats. Alternative means for exercising power—that is, alternative means of "reason giving" in the noumenal space of power—include moving public speeches, insightful personal recommendations, novel redescriptions of the world, verbal commands, and even acts of seduction.[8] Pointing a gun at someone remains, for Forst, a powerful "reason" for that person to consider modifying his or her thought or behavior, but it is not, by any stretch, the only available form of justification.

By expanding the repertoire of the means of exercising power, Forst concomitantly expands our conceptualization of its *effects:* not merely does someone who threatens us exercise power over us, but so too, in the noumenal conception, do those who persuade or seduce us. It remains an open question whether those who persuade or seduce us, even threaten us, have motivated us into doing something that benefits or harms us. The point is precisely that the question remains open: domination and subordination are not the only possible outcomes of the exercise of power. Enlightenment, pleasure, and liberation are also possible outcomes in the exercise of noumenal power.

There are, to my mind, two key elements to Forst's noumenal conception of power that, if not necessarily normative in and of themselves, nevertheless harbor deeply normative implications. The first is the assumption on the part of the actor exercising power that the intended subject of power possesses a free will and is capable of making choices among alternative courses of action. In this sense, even someone who intends to dominate or subordinate another person, at least implicitly, understands the other to be an *agent*. The second is that the subject of power must accept the justifications provided by the wielder of power for changing their own thought or behavior. If the subject of power does *not* accept these justifications and therefore fails to modify their subsequent thought or behavior, then *no* power has been exercised over them. Indeed, according to Forst, when the actor who threatens the use of force resorts to the *actual* use of force in the face of a recalcitrant, prospective subject of power, they have actually lost power over the subject.

Through such arguments, Forst exposes the fact that "realist" theorists of power conceptually treat subjects of power as manipulable objects and not as thinking subjects who respond—or refuse to respond—to reasons and justifications. Furthermore, realists fail to recognize the distinction between the *threat* of physical force and the *act* of physical force. For Forst, even threats operate within the realm of justification because they grant the subject of power the opportunity to respond or not respond to the reasons or justifications for mental or behavioral modification provided by the would-be power-wielder. The moment that the would-be power-wielder resorts to actual physical force is the moment when they are least powerful. It is worth quoting Rainer at length here:

> A threat gives the person who is threatened a reason to do something, but as long as a relation of power exists, at least one alternative way of acting is open to the person threatened. Otherwise this person would be a mere object, like a stone or a tree that is being moved. Thus, a case of pure force, where A moves B purely by physical means, by handcuffing him or her and carrying him or her away, is no longer an exercise of power, for the handcuffed person doesn't "do" anything; rather, something "is done" to him or her. At that point, power as a relation between agents turns into brute physical force and violence, and the noumenal character vanishes.[9]

This is a rather eloquent elaboration of what we might call a "phenomenology of power," one in which power fully negates itself when it resorts to actual physical force.

I could go on plumbing the depths of Forst's fascinating and provocative noumenal conception of power. Here let me address some tensions and ambiguities that, it seems to me, inhere within the theory.

3. INTENTIONALITY AND NOUMENAL POWER

There are two ambiguities, as I see them: one undermines the capaciousness of Forst's conception;[10] the other suggests that the conception may be *too* capacious to serve as an effective means of analysis in the realm of politics. Readers will readily observe that these remarks— really queries more than criticisms—pull Forst in two diametrically opposed directions.

First, with how much specificity must a subject of power think or act in a manner intended by a power-wielder for a relation of noumenal power to obtain? That is, for Forst, how precisely must a subject of power think or act in conformity with a power-wielder's intentions? Indeed, how determinate, in the first place, must the power-wielder's intentions be for any consequent thought or action to be considered the result of an exercise of noumenal power? As I read it, Forst's definition suggests that the concept entails a fairly strong, determinate notion of intentionality, but his examples do not necessarily bear out the necessity of strong, precise intentions on the part of power-wielders.

Forst sometimes distinguishes between, on the one hand, *power,* the exercise of which entails hard intentionality on the part of a power wielder, from, on the other, *influence,* an action behind which no specific intention motivates the initiating actor.[11] But Forst himself often treats influence as a subset of power[12]—sometimes on the very same page where he distinguishes between the two phenomena.[13]

Second, do conditions of noumenal power apply if a power-wielder effects a change *only* in the mental state of a subject of power? Or must such a subjective change be accompanied by a resulting change in *behavior* on the part of the subject for a relation of noumenal power to apply? If Forst is satisfied with effecting a change *only* in the mental states of subjects of power, does this water down the meaning of political power, which is usually associated with the ability of power-wielders to motivate or prevent concrete actions on the part of subjects of power?

Regarding intentionality, I wonder whether Forst unnecessarily imports a falsely realist element from the Weberian conception of power into his own noumenal conception. Forst writes, "To be a subject of power is to be moved by reasons that others have given me and that motivate me to think *or* act in a certain way *intended by the reason-giver.*"[14] Forst here builds into the definition of noumenal power the condition that the *intention* of the power-wielder must be successfully realized in the changed thought or actions of the subject. But I think that Forst's own arguments for including acts of persuasion—and even seduction—under the rubric of exercises of noumenal power do not necessitate the thick notion of intentionality implied by Forst's definition. I want to raise the possibility that Forst might want to relax the condition of intentionality—or at least that he might consider presenting it in a more differentiated way.

It seems to me that the wielder of noumenal power need not intend for the subject of power to *do* anything in particular: he or she may be ultimately indifferent about what the subject actually does. Her power resides simply in the expanding or limiting of the mental horizon of possibilities experienced by the subject (for good or ill). She already exercises power at the moment when the subject recognizes, in a way that he hasn't before, that he can or should (or cannot or should not) think or act in a certain way on the basis of the reasons provided by the power-wielder.

If, for instance, pedagogy counts as a form of persuasion, then teachers exercise power all the time over students by fundamentally changing (or even by ever so slightly expanding) the latter's view of the world. In many such cases, teachers are agnostic concerning what their students actually do with—or as a result of—this altered worldview (although we certainly hope for the best). There is, in such cases, at most a soft intentionality manifested in the attempt to effect an internal change upon the subjects of power (in this case, our students) but not necessarily the hard intentionality implied by Forst regarding any subsequent or consequent mental state or external behavior on the subjects' part. A student may, after all, subsequently return to a previously held belief, but they do, albeit temporarily, change his or her mental state. The status of the *change* effected is in some sense ambiguous in such cases: the student has entertained both "old" and "new" beliefs, even if he reverts to the old ones.

Similarly, noumenal power in the form of seduction need not entail as much strong intentionality on the part of a would-be wielder of power as it might first appear or as Forst seems to imply. Strong intentionality, in fact, applies only to the most crassly mechanical definitions of seduction, to which Forst clearly does not subscribe.

Quite plausibly, the intention of someone engaged in an act of seduction is not necessarily to convince someone else to engage in sexual activity with him. Rather, it may be an exploration, initiated by one agent but—crucially—subsequently engaged in by *both* agents, regarding the intentions of both parties. No definite outcome is necessarily pursued on the part of *either* actor. Most importantly for the noumenal concept of power: only a *possible* and not a *definite* change in the thought or action of the subject of power is intended by the agent when she initiates what Forst eloquently—and suggestively, when applied to this case—calls "a certain relation in the space of justifications."[15]

Alternatively, if a power-wielder *is* motivated by a stronger kind of intentionality when he or she initiates an act of seduction, his or her efforts at reason giving are highly provisional. Seduction constitutes the attempt of one party to persuade another party to share his worldview on a specific matter, but if the attempt at forging such a shared worldview fails, then, in this case, the initiator of the relation of power *ceases* in his effort to effect a change in the mental or behavioral condition of the would-be subject of power. Otherwise, seduction becomes something else entirely. Seduction does indeed conform to Forst's concept of noumenal power, but it may be something of a limit case of noumenal power.[16]

Perhaps this understanding of seduction is ridiculously naïve or hopelessly romantic. The point I'm trying to make is that seduction often entails (1) considerable ambivalence in the intentions of the power-wielder, (2) radical freedom of choice on the part of the subject of power, and (3) ultimately, wild indeterminacy in the outcome of the ensuing relation in the space of justifications (whether this manifests itself in mental states or in concrete behavior). However, I believe that it still counts as a form of noumenal power, according to Forst's conception, if not exactly in the way that Forst articulates his notion of intentionality (and maybe his notion of "effected change" as well).

Forst might well respond to these examples that problematize intentionality with the following rejoinder: the noumenal concept of power explicitly counts *any* successful attempt, however tentative or unconsidered, by one party to motivate a change, however slight or minimally efficacious, in another party's intellectual or emotional condition as constituting an example of power-wielding. Soft intentionality that effects even minor changes in the psychic state of subjects (whether or not subjects subsequently *act* or *behave* in a way that the power-wielders even remotely intend) is fully compatible with the conception of noumenal power. When the intention to effect a change, of whatever magnitude, in the mind, heart, or soul of another party has been realized, then the conditions of noumenal power have been satisfied.

4. POWER OVER THOUGHT AND/OR ACTION?

This then leads into the second ambiguity mentioned earlier. Forst's satisfaction with situations in which power-wielders effect changes exclusively in the mental states—and not necessarily in the behavior—of subjects is fully in keeping with the compelling capaciousness of his model of noumenal power. However, this capaciousness runs the risk of blunting the efficacy of Forst's model in the effort to analyze politics—a realm in which inducements to *act* (or not to act) on the part of power-wielders and empirically observable instances of *action* (or inaction) on the part of subjects of power are crucial.

I invite Forst to consider whether, to what extent, or under what conditions he might consider constricting his notion of noumenal power to account for changes not merely in the mental states of subjects of power but more specifically in the actions of such subjects. I prompt him to explore more thoroughly how noumenal power operates in the realm of thought *versus* the realm of action and whether a change in *behavior* on the part of subjects is somehow required for noumenal power to have greater theoretical purchase within the political realm. In short, Forst needs to consider whether the kind of power exercised by, say, teachers, mentioned earlier, differs fundamentally from the kind of power exercised by police officers or soldiers.

Another way of making the point more dramatically is to ask the question in a way that combines both of the ambiguities that I've been discussing: Does the *political* application of noumenal power require subjects of power to *act* concretely in a way more or less precisely *intended* by the wielder of power? Is there a *hard* character to the exercise of noumenal *political* power regarding intentions *and* actions that is not characteristic of the exercise of noumenal power in realms primarily characterized by changes in thought or feeling? Does Forst want to narrow the concept of noumenal power to apply only to those cases where a change in *both* the thought *and* the actions of the subject occur? These are genuinely open questions.

I would prefer not to conclude this section on the side of theoretical parsimony; I would much rather accentuate the capaciousness of noumenal power. As Forst rightly reminds us, "We need to keep in mind the different degrees of the exercise of noumenal power."[17] Moreover, it is a strength not a weakness of Forst's concept of noumenal power that it remains open to "ambivalence and contestation" concerning the intentions and motivations of both agents and subjects of power: "Even though I warned at the outset against the metaphysical idea of noumenal 'things in themselves,' there is some truth to this way of speaking. For, as Kant remarked, we cannot look into the heads of people in order to discover which reasons actually motivate them. Thus, in a way, any analysis of noumenal power has to accept *ambivalence and contestation*; it can never be final and completely objective."[18] Allow me to use an example, not from Immanuel Kant but from Machiavelli, to illustrate the ambiguities of subjective intentions/motivations and the indeterminacy of objective outcomes in the exercise of noumenal power. In both the *Discourses* and the *Florentine Histories,* Machiavelli discusses the example of Countess Caterina Sforza of Forlì.[19]

In 1488, conspirators wishing to take over the city of Forlì kidnap Sforza and her children. The countess convinces the kidnappers to permit her to enter the citadel in order to command her soldiers to surrender. The conspirators continue to hold her children hostage as a guarantee that Sforza will comply with their demands. Upon entering the fortress, Sforza climbs the ramparts and addresses the kidnappers from the heights of its walls. She raises her skirt, exposing her genitals to her enemies, and tells them to go ahead and kill her children because she can make more. Stunned and dismayed, the usurpers flee, leaving Sforza's children unharmed and leaving the countess in complete control of the city.

I have no doubt that Sforza intended to exert noumenal power over the kidnappers in this episode. She intended to insult and humiliate them by simultaneously flouting and exalting gendered expectations over what counted as socially acceptable behavior for women in her day. She engaged in a lewd act usually associated with ostentatious displays of masculine sexual prowess, defied conventional notions concerning how mothers are expected to feel about their children, and exploited male fear and envy of feminine procreative power. She quite successfully accomplished her goal of embarrassing her adversaries. However, since she had already regained the city for herself, her behavior here is, in at least one sense, gratuitous. The question is, Could she really have expected to rescue her children in the process of humiliating her enemies? Such are the ambiguities of intentions and outcomes in the exercise of noumenal power.

5. LATERAL EFFECTS IN THE MULTIACTOR GAME OF POLITICS

One of the most appealing cryptonormative aspects of Forst's ostensibly nonnormative, noumenal conception of power is the way that it attributes agency to the subjects of power. In Forst's conception, even victims of the most egregious forms of physical intimidation maintain their human dignity as rational agents who are capable of exercising a free, albeit difficult, choice between compliance or pain. Forst makes an observation meant to confirm the fact that *both* reason giving by power-wielders *and* free, if excruciating, choice making by power-targets constitute the normal conditions—and not exceptional situations—within the realm of politics, but I suspect that it may, in fact, confirm the opposite. Forst writes, "The person moved by sheer force is . . . completely under the control of the other, as a mere physical object, and so, seen in isolation from noumenal-social contexts, [he or she] is no longer an agent in the relevant sense. But such isolation is artificial, *for most of the time* an exercise of physical force is meant to have a noumenal effect either on the person subjected to it (for example, of instilling fear) or on others who witness what is going on."[20] I accentuate the phrase "most of the time" because the unintended ambiguity with which Forst employs it here bespeaks the potential limited scope of noumenal power in the realm of politics. The realm of politics may not be—and cannot be—an entirely noumenal realm of power wielding by means of reason giving. Politics may necessarily entail, most of the time, the treatment of individuals, groups, or large swaths of populations *not* as free rational agents but as mere physical objects—if only, as Forst concedes earlier, to provide other subjects of power strong motivations to alter their own behavior.

Michel Foucault gave the name "lateral effects" to this phenomenon, one that Machiavelli long before considered to be the very essence of politics. The act of spectacularly executing a single individual or some larger portion of the population—not only to frighten but, in Machiavelli's case, also to please the generality of the population—conforms very closely to what Machiavelli calls "cruelty well-used."

A prince or even a republic *must* treat some subjects or citizens as objects in order to guarantee the stability and even the justice of the polity. Since some political actors will invariably threaten the rule of the prince or the liberty of the people, they will consistently pose a problem to order as would-be usurpers and to justice as agents seeking to oppress large portions of the population—persons that they are prevented from fully oppressing under the status quo. The spectacular execution of a single usurper or an oligarchic clique, whom Machiavelli called "the sons of Brutus," serves three purposes: it eliminates a grave, clear, and present danger; it deters future mischief on the part of would-be usurpers cum oppressors; and it satisfies the general populace with a concrete demonstration that the present regime will vigorously defend their security or their liberty.

Foucault, of course, through the example of Damien's torture and execution at the outset of *Discipline and Punish,* demonstrated how such spectacles of political punishment can go spectacularly wrong for wielders of power.[21] Instead of an example that deters would-be regicides and keeps the common people on the side of the king, Damien becomes a popular hero. Moreover, instead of the victim of unendurable pain, Damien enjoys the best day of his life—being induced into religio-erotic ecstasy by the state's protractedly botched efforts at dismembering and burning his body.

The rest of Foucault's book is more sobering in its demonstration that mundane forms of discipline and punishment are constitutive aspects of modern politics. This insight is, of course, more relevant in the age of the incarceration state than it was when Foucault first published the book. Machiavelli preferred power-wielders to incarcerate or execute society's predatory elites; Foucault reminds us, on the contrary, that modern regimes, even the most supposedly liberal-democratic of them, deprive of life and liberty massive numbers of their poor and powerless populations. This is precisely the mode of governing that Machiavelli identified as "cruelty badly used." Yet whomever the targets of brute, naked power may be, oppressive elites or defenseless populaces, Machiavelli and Foucault insist—Rainer Forst's estimable efforts notwithstanding—that some number of society, rightly or wrongly, must suffer objectifying force so that the rest of us may live in "a certain relation within the space of justifications"—that is, so that we might continue to think and act as subjects of noumenal power.

NOTES

For comments and criticisms, I thank Chiara Cordelli, Steven Klein, Ian Storey, and especially my commentator, Pablo Gilabert.

1. Rainer Forst, "Noumenal Power," *Journal of Political Philosophy* 23, no. 2 (2015): 111–27. References conform to the pagination of the online version of the essay.
2. Amy Allen, *The End of Progress: Decolonizing the Normative Foundations of Critical Theory* (New York: Columbia University Press, 2016).

3. Max Weber, *Economy and Society,* trans. and ed. G. Roth and C. Wittich (Los Angeles: University of California Press, 1978).

4. Forst, "Noumenal Power," 1.

5. Ibid.

6. Ibid., 2.

7. Ibid.

8. Ibid., 5.

9. Ibid.

10. For views on the merits and limits of a capacious notion of power that bear on Forst's concept of noumenal power, see Amy Allen, Rainer Forst, and Mark Haugaard, "Power and Reason, Justice and Domination: A Conversation," *Journal of Political Power* 7, no. 1 (2014): 7–33; Pablo Gilabert, "A Broad Definition of Agential Power," *Journal of Political Power* 11, no. 1 (2018): 79–92.

11. Forst, "Noumenal Power," 10, 14. For instance, Forst writes, "It is, however, more appropriate to speak of 'influence' rather than 'power' in cases where power is not intentionally exercised by persons over others" (120); and further, "We call power generally the capacity of A to influence the space of reasons for B and/or C (etc.) such that they think and act in ways they would not have done without the interference by A; moreover, the move by A must have a motivating force for B and/or C (etc.) that corresponds to A's intentions and is not just a side effect (i.e., a form of influence)" (124).

12. Ibid., 6, 11.

13. Ibid., 10, 14.

14. Ibid., 2 (italics added).

15. Ibid., 6.

16. See ibid., 15–16. Another potentially interesting limit case discussed by Forst is torture. He writes, "At that moment [when torture is deployed], power as a normative force moving an even minimally free agent fades away; it might reappear when those subjected to violence begin to act as the power-wielder wills, either out of fear or because they are traumatized, but, in any case, no longer as mere physical objects." In the case of torture, then, power wielders often alternate between the deployment of objectifying violence that denies subjects their agency and noumenal reason giving that affirms it. In this case, power is only intermittently noumenal.

17. Ibid., 14. In this spirit, he writes further, "We have to analyze power relations along a spectrum extending from its exercise through the justificatory quality of reasons shared among deliberating persons, at one end, to the limiting case of its exercise by way of physical force, at the other, which in its extreme form lies outside of the realm of power, being instead a reflection of the lack of power. The reality of the exercise of power usually falls somewhere in between"; see ibid., 16.

18. Ibid., 16 (italics added).

19. Niccolò Machiavelli, *Discourses* (London: Penguin, 2003), book 3, discourse 6; Niccolò Machiavelli, *Florentine Histories,* trans. Laura F. Banfield and Harvey C. Mansfield (Princeton: Princeton University Press, 1988), book 8, chap. 34.

20. Forst, "Noumenal Power," 5 (italics added).

21. Michel Foucault, *Discipline & Punish: The Birth of the Prison,* trans. A. Sheridan (New York: Pantheon, 1978), 3–6.

CHAPTER 7

Opening "Political Contexts of Injustice"

Melissa Yates

Claims of injustice are special, and what we do to invite and empower them in our political communities is crucial for democratic progress. In reflecting on global poverty, Rainer Forst warns against "using good moral arguments at the wrong place" to emphasize the danger of converting injustice into a matter for benevolence or generosity, humanism or solidarity.[1] He invites us to extrapolate from a photograph in Sebastião Salgado's series "The Gold Mine Portfolio."[2] In the 1980s, the giant Serra Pelada mine bulged as nearly one hundred thousand men dug through the mud, searching for gold. The Brazilian government operated the mine, paying workers pitifully for their findings and price gouging them on supplies such as water. The few that hit the jackpot with big finds fueled the hopes of the tens of thousands who scraped by. Serra Pelada drew from economically desperate populations and exploited them through appalling work conditions, though they were not forced to work in the mine. Many were killed by the dangerous work conditions or murdered for their findings, and those who survived were exposed to mercury poisoning. Forst's thought experiment walks us through possible ways a goldmine worker might make a claim to injustice through the counsel of expert theorists, each of which inadequately seeks to translate the worker's injustice claim into a different kind of moral claim. Though the example resonates as unjust, the full scope of the injustice depends on the loosening of our grip on the scope of political power. Instead, a critical theory of injustice, Forst argues, relies on the historical causes and social-scientifically represented realities of the situation, focusing on the context of injustice rather than strictly on poverty or individual harms in isolation.[3] This requires seeing relationships of power structured by domination and violence, rather than merely seeing the absence or deprivation of goods. To be recognized as entitled to advance a claim of injustice requires that the claimant be seen in the context of political relationships of power. But many contexts of injustice arise precisely in conditions where political relationships and their stakes and impacts are veiled.

To count as someone subjected to political power reflects his or her status as a member of a political community with some visibility and standing. It is a precondition of the crucial question, Is the political power to which I am subjected justified? The question itself concerns the boundary of who counts as a member of a political community and, beyond that, what full membership entails.[4] But the other side of this question about *who* counts is a boundary question of a different kind: *Which forms of power* should count as political? What's primarily at stake in this second way of thinking about boundaries is whether we open discourses about justice or legitimacy to forms of power that run their course through extralegal channels. Being a subject of political power (the membership question) depends on how we define what counts as an exercise of political power to begin with (the ontopolitical question). If political power includes forms of rule and domination through economic, social, cultural, or transnational forms of power, then our account of membership groups of political communities needs to be adjusted to fit the scope of power.

Forst's work on both questions is remarkably helpful in pushing forward the evolution of this topic, and I am broadly sympathetic to much about his approach. In the spirit of Forst's crafting of multidimensional titles, I intend for my own title to have two meanings. The first meaning is, hopefully, straightforward: I'm interested in ways that Forst himself has opened, or widened, what he calls "political contexts of injustice" to include, among others, transnational contexts. The second meaning of my title speaks to the normative precommitments and implications that implicitly guide political relationships and our politicization of practices of power. Redefining political boundaries of membership and standing raises questions about which norms are compatible with efforts to "make space" for newcomers or newly visible members. So on the one hand, I'm interested in Forst's opening of the social ontological boundaries of political communities, and on the other, I'm interested in the ways his norms of democratization guide our openness to those who are and will be new members.

I would like to pursue three aims: In the first section, I provide an analysis of what defines a political community for Forst, focusing on his ideas of contexts of justice and the right to justifications and his argument regarding justice as tracking relations of power. Here I interpret Forst's position as one of challenging us to open what we count as contexts of injustice. In the second section, I argue that Forst's work on the issue of transnational injustice (and, possibly, on what he calls "contexts of multiple domination") might be fruitfully extended more deeply into a temporal dimension of the boundary problem, in terms of what I shall call *transtemporal* relations of political power. I then consider reasons for and against the compatibility of transtemporal contexts of justice and injustice in Forst's sense. In the third section, I raise questions about whether, despite opening contexts of injustice, Forst's account of argumentation according to the right to justification can sufficiently "make space" for the inclusion of new, unfamiliar, foreign, evolving members.

1. OPENNESS OF POLITICAL COMMUNITIES

To speak of the idea of more or less *open* accounts of political communities is a bit out of sync with the way Forst characterizes his own view, so I want to begin with a brief explanation about why I think the open/closed characterization applies well to Forst's account and to sketch the kinds of problems the evocation of the idea of "openness" speaks to. The meaning of openness as I'm using it seems to fit well with Forst's use of (what he calls) a *dereified* version of democracy as a practice of democratization; so for the purpose of this section,

I plan to explore openness as a practice of democratization. Along with other political philosophical concepts such as justice and liberty, Forst transforms "democracy" from a somewhat stable or passive thing with material footings in formal institutions into democratic practices. Forst summarizes, "[Democracy consists in] a political practice of argumentation and reason-giving among free and equal citizens, a practice in which individual and collective perspectives and positions are subject to change through deliberation and in which only those norms, rules, or decisions that result from some form of reason-based agreement among the citizens are accepted as legitimate."[5] His approach guides the underlying motivation for openness, as I use the term, in conceiving political communities. He expands on this in "Transnational Justice and Non-domination," where he describes practices of democratization as follows: "The recuperation of relations of rule and domination and their transformation into relations of justification is rightly called 'democratization' when it succeeds in generating structures that successfully challenge arbitrary rule, for instance through effective 'contestation.' . . . Whenever privileged actors are forced to surrender their prerogatives because these have lost their legitimation—after exposure to criticism within a system of justification and the formation of counter-power—this represents an increase in democracy."[6]

Openness as democratization fundamentally involves exposing status-quo assumptions about political relations of power to critique. Since democratization seeks out unjustified relations of power, it also involves an opening of political communities to broader ways of conceiving political power. When we are ruled or dominated through economic, social, or cultural tools of political power (extralegally, let's say), the idea of a political community has to be wide enough and flexible enough to accommodate discourses critically reflecting on and seeking to transform those relations. Democratization first involves attending to relations of rule and domination that are unjustified, wherever the rule or domination appears. Forst emphasizes, "Who dominates whom? *That* defines where the borders of a context of justice as justification lie."[7] This is why for him a theory of justice realistically requires a "complex theory of injustice,"[8] because "most often contexts of justice are contexts of injustice first."[9] Since "justice in political

contexts demands that there are no social relations 'beyond justification,'"[10] according to Forst, the first priority of justice is to end arbitrary
rule and domination, not merely (or primarily) through redistributing
goods but by reforming the relationships of justification themselves
such that all subjected to political power are treated as beings with a
right to justification.[11]

We can distinguish between three ways that democratization,
as Forst seems to use it, implies opening our ideas about political
communities:

(a) The breadth or variety of forms/domains of power that
count as political power have to be opened such that contexts of injustice can be "recuperated" and "transformed."

(b) The extent of beings who can be counted as members
of political communities have to be opened through
democratization by expanding the reach of those who
have standing, and who are thus owed justifications.

(c) There needs to be sufficient flexibility regarding the
accepted or established boundaries of (a) and (b) in any
status quo such that both the forms power takes and
those who are subjected are a matter of constant investigation and amendment.

Before weighing how these each play out in complex cases, it will
likely help to pull together what I take to be the broader background
for attributing each claim to Forst's view, particularly so that he can
more easily identify places where I've misunderstood the connections
between and across his works.

a. Openness in the Forms/Domains of Political Power

Political communities are political communities of justification for
Forst, where generality and reciprocity serve as the measures of justification of norms in contexts of justification.[12] We find ourselves
in political communities of justification wherever political power
is exercised through rule or domination, but he argues that political

communities of justification are "often not coextensive with established political communities."[13] Instead, the political context of justice "'tracks' power as rule or domination."[14] As a consequence, democratization requires that the forms and tools adopted by political power be defined in multiform ways to provide adequate recognition of injustice wherever it appears and to leave us with an agile-enough critical theory to track down and analyze forms of power that work outside traditional legal or narrowly civic-political contexts.

Forst's approach in terms of a critical theory of contexts of injustice begins in the empirical world of ruled and dominated beings. But "power," "rule," and "domination" have particular meanings for Forst, which set limits on the expectations of democratization. With respect to power, Forst is committed to a noumenal interpretation, which he thinks coheres with his overall strategy of dereifying political philosophical concepts.[15] Power is noumenal in the sense of influencing the space of reasons available to others such that they think and act differently than they otherwise would have thought or acted. For Forst, the account of political power is woven into his broader account of justification: "Power should be understood in processual terms as the ability to determine, or if necessary even to close off (or also to open up), the space of reasons for others, whether based on a good argument, an ideological justification, or a threat. Social power does not have its 'seat' in some means, institutions, or structures, but instead in the noumenal space in which struggles over hegemony take place."[16] Power identifies processes by which we either negatively or positively influence the space of reasons for others. It is compatible with justice and is not necessarily arbitrary. Both the ideas of rule and domination spell out specific instantiations and ways of operationalizing power in political contexts. Rule is an especially important example of the senses in which Forst uses power as a neutral term, because although being ruled constrains us, in defining and limiting the space of reasons for us, that constraint alone does not amount to unjustifiable or oppressive constraint in the case of democratic rule. Rule represents a form of power where the ways that power-holders influence the space of reasons are based on more or less comprehensive justifications. Power as rule draws from resources in religious, moral, metaphysical, or historical justifications in framing the social or political relationships in a social order. The durability of rule seems decisive in distinguishing its importance as a potentially enabling form of power. Rule structures what we in practice expect from ourselves and others in terms of justification. Our spaces of reason are inevitably socially and historically constrained in many ways (often ways invisible to us), but members of social orders under democratic rule are enabled by those structures insofar as their dual role as addressee and author of social and political power is only possible under conditions of rule.

In contrast to rule, Forst uses the idea of domination to pick out forms of power exercised in contexts lacking structures of justification to critically reflect on and contest the justifications of power.[17] Power as domination reflects the absence of a structured way to develop and test reciprocally and generally justifiable norms; in this way, domination is antithetical to democratic rule, which involves the creation and support for structures that provide just those kinds of discursive arenas. Importantly, power exercised through domination need not be imaginatively restricted to extreme forms of authoritarianism. Benevolent domination is still domination in that the power depends on a view of the relationship of power out of step with my full status as a justifying being, instead only appealing one-sidedly to my status as a receiver of justification. In domination I am addressed merely as the addressee of exercises of power without the ability to see myself as the author of the norms that bind me.

But both rule and domination express forms of power exercised with some connection to creating and contributing to the spaces of reason (otherwise they wouldn't count as "power" in Forst's sense).[18] In contrast, when spaces of justification are entirely absent—and instead replaced with exercises of brute force—then such exercises are forms of violence. Under conditions of violence, beings are reduced to "things," and my status and significance as a justifying being is wholly closed off and denied.[19]

Returning to the question of how we can understand the extent to which political domains are open for Forst, his argument that justice tracks exercises of power means that social orders broadly and multiply understood are political whenever power holders exercise rule or domination. So in the case of the goldmine worker constructing claims of injustice, the pressures of justification rightly apply to more than just nation-state laws of Brazil; his claim to injustice applies to the global economic social order, and possibly the cultural social order that structure his standing in relationships of power. This leads to the second component of defining political spaces—namely, the question of how we define the political agency of the beings in those relationships of power.

b. Openness in Terms of Democratization of Membership

A view of political membership can be more or less open by reference to what it takes to be fundamental about the qualifications for counting as a member.[20] In Forst's view, "not being viewed as someone others owe reasons to" is worse than "the insult of being treated unjustifiably."[21] The combination of Forst's account of the forms of political power and of persons as justifying beings suggests a response to my question about political community membership conditions. Relationships of power exercised through rule or domination inhere between members of social orders, in Forst's sense. You can't make sense of processes of justification going on within relationships of power without also extending something like membership status to the beings in the relationship—though that membership status need not be recognized appropriately, as in cases of domination. That means as we widen the forms of power that count as appropriate targets for democratization, we are at the same time widening our account of who should count as members of political communities. If an environmental law passed in the United States exercises power over people beyond its borders, then with the extension of power comes the membership rights, and we can use that connection to argue in favor of democratization of that power by, among other things, making visible the people who are ruled and dominated but not counted and creating institutions that invite those who have a right to justification into new arenas of discourse to test the exercises of power that bind us across traditional legal borders.

But in cases like the goldmine worker or cases where we don't really have evidence that a person is being treated like a justifying being at all, then Forst would likely understand the case as an exercise of violence instead of power. At this point, we can think either that political communities should be restricted to exercises of already recognized political power or that you can be a member of a political community even though the structures and relationships between people entirely deny that any such community exists. It's often a tool of violence to deny political standing (and more widely, moral standing) to people who stand in political relationships with those inflicting violence. While violence can't erase the existence of qualities that makes relationships politicizable, it can all but eliminate practical means to act as if we stand in political relationships or to advance claims of injustice. These are precisely the cases that deserve the gaze of critical theorists, who can politicize relationships between people and within social structures by personalizing the members of the relationships—in other words, in contexts of violence, much of the initial work of democratization just is seeing relationships as political and seeing people as people (or as justifying beings).

c. Openness in Terms of Ongoing Flexibility and Amendability of Boundaries

In analyzing sites of power effective in our social contexts, we implicitly identify a relationship of power—those who are subjects and those who are authors. For Forst, it's important to begin with contexts in which power is unjustly wielded. This is unpacked in what he calls the maxim of "first things first." A critical theory of injustice consists in a critique of existing relations of justification. Such a theory has three goals: to expose unjustifiable social relations that exclude or dominate through exercises of power in a wide political sense (including economic or cultural unjustifiable social relations).

I'm inclined to see this point in terms of social relations becoming politicized whenever members effectively opt for the political tools of rule or domination. Where there is a ruled and ruler (individual or collective), there is a political relationship, regardless of whether these relationships also map onto traditionally extrapolitical situations, such as between members of a church congregation or players on a soccer team. The sense in which "effective" rule or domination comes into play might help relieve concerns that every relationship could be viewed in a political light; there is likely some general resistance within social relationships to accept attempts at politicization. But where political relationships of power have successfully structured the options and choices of those subjected to that power, then I see no reason to rule them out (I think I'm in agreement with Forst here).

A view could be more or less open in terms of its flexibility, and I think that Forst's idea of democratization invites significant openness as revisability and flexibility, particularly insofar as he tasks critical theorists with the work of identifying veiled and otherwise invisible relations of power and of critiquing with an aim to transform those relations. That will be an ongoing task, and in doing so, we necessarily shift between the form of power and the membership of political communities. An adjustment in one reverberates to the other. I'm generally sympathetic to a wide view that includes many different kinds of rule and, by implication, many dimensions of membership in political communities. But the question of whether the political community is fairly settled over time, whether it needs some kind of group identity, suggests a different kind of openness. If the act of designating members and scopes of political communities amounts to a form of rule and identity constitution, then it would seem that changes depend on the willingness of those who already have the benefits of membership.

But the view that anything can be politicized and thereby be appropriately evaluated in light of justice and legitimacy does not mean that we can or should politicize all relationships. To use a Forstian processual account of the politicization of power could mean not that relationships themselves are either political or apolitical but rather that the ways that power structures relationships are always open to political evaluations and, in that way, are politicizable. That violence against one's spouse is rightly politicizable does not depend on our seeing the relationship between spouses as inherently political, nor does it mean that politicizing violence requires the wholesale politicizing of a relationship.[22]

But there might be another kind of overopenness risk: for contexts of injustice to apply, we first have to be able to be related to each other in politically meaningful ways. That seems to return us to the issue of conditions for political agency. So the way the river "rules" my options on a hike doesn't reflect an obvious relationship of power, since the river isn't a justifying being and can't actually rule or dominate me, even if we speak metaphorically in those terms. Politicizing the way that my options are reduced or enabled by river considerations (placement, speed, freshness/cleanliness) requires that I find or attribute to political agents the relationships of power at work. If the river is man-made or if the river is polluted from factories dumping waste into it, then what's going on with a river can be politicized without adopting the idea of relationships with rivers.

2. TRANSTEMPORAL OPENNESS

Forst's account of justice consists in processes that improve the democratization of relations of power. Democracy applies to "all domains of exercising rule, including economic relations, both national and transnational."[23] Since democracy is not definitionally tied to states or nations, or formal institutions, for Forst a claim to political or social justice is a claim to democratic justice. In particular, political power that extends beyond national borders raises questions of transnational claims to justice. I'm interested in a parallel series of questions, regarding the possibility of temporal limits of political relationships and on the implications of what I will refer to as "transtemporal" political relationships of power for Forst's account of justification. Can we be ruled or dominated by members of our political community who entirely preexist us, or can we dominate those to come? Reciprocity and justification seem to depend on restricting one's understanding of political relationships to those with whom we share "our time," but in many respects, we seem to stand in relationships of power, in Forst's own sense of power, with people who precede and follow us.

With respect to questions about how we might understand political relationships with persons who preexist us, political theorists have raised questions about whether it's possible to democratically legitimate constitutional principles that we are precommitted to, given that our very ability to legitimate political power depends on the institutions and safeguards created by the very constitutional principles and basic laws that we seek to legitimate.[24] I think that regardless of the strategies adopted into or out of such a paradox, the underlying presence of a problem of precommitment reflects the potential usefulness of opening our account of membership to include a transtemporal political relationship between those who through rule, domination, and violence still enable and constrain our spaces of reason. Alternately, it seems that part of democratization requires that we endeavor to precommit those to come to spaces of reason that provide them with the ability to stand in relationships of power with each other as justifying beings. In creating durable structures that enable the kinds of justification discourses Forst has in mind, we have to see ourselves as precommitting others. Now the question, I think, for Forst will be whether the ways that we precommit them can be rejected by them on grounds of failing to be reciprocally and generally justifiable. So the kinds of examples I have in mind would be subject to justification discourses over time that test precisely whether they are or continue to be rejectable in those ways.

At this point, it likely helps to see more clearly the kinds of transtemporal political relationships I think we can make sense of, where we could make a case for the usefulness of politicizing the rule and domination of some from the past over others now. Consider the following four examples:

- In 1938, the United States passed the Fair Labor Standards Act (FLSA) with major concessions to Southern Democrats at the time. Since then, the law has continued to exclude agricultural and domestic workers (who were then and continue to be mostly nonwhite) from labor protections extended to workers in other markets, including minimum-wage standards and overtime pay, and continues to prevent laborers in these markets from forming unions, contributing to deep poverty and poor work conditions among both groups of workers across generations. For instance, as recently as 2011, 75 percent of farmworkers earned less than $10,000 annually.[25]
- In 1804, the U.S. Congress passed the Twelfth Amendment, which revised (while basically readopting) the original constitutional design of the electoral college. Since then, the Twelfth

Amendment has applied to every U.S. presidential election, including the 2016 election in which Donald Trump won the electoral-college votes while losing the popular vote.

- In 1911, the U.S. Congress passed the Apportionment Act of 1911, which capped the number of representatives in the House of Representatives at 435. Voters in low-population states now have significantly more weight in deciding presidential elections than voters in high-population states. For example, voters in Wyoming have 3.6 times the voting weight as voters in California.[26]
- In 1922, U.S. Congress failed to pass the NAACP-backed Dyer Bill, proposed in 1918. The antilynching law sought to provide federal recourse in response to the widespread lynching of African Americans during the Jim Crow era by white terrorists. Nearly four thousand African Americans were lynched between 1880 and 1950, a high percentage of whom were business owners and leaders who resisted white oppression, the effects of which still arguably harm the social, economic, and political power of African American communities.[27]

Each of these cases seems ripe for democratization, which I think would involve our recuperating the hierarchies of power that then and now enable them to rule or dominate us. Seeing our predecessors as standing in relationships with us more clearly invites and prompts the discourses of justification that Forst has in mind. While we can't have those discourses with predecessors, working through anew and on a continuing basis the justifications (or absences of justifications) for precommitment seems to be a crucial part of Forst's wider sense of democratic progress. Identifying political relationships with predecessors need not undermine our sense of responsibility for continuing to be complicit over time in ways that enable the past to have such continued power over us. Indeed, spotlighting their continued role as actively shaping our present would seem to empower the present. The emphasis is generally on ferreting out forms of domination in an effort to democratize those forms of power. But even if that is the priority, failing to take up the work of reevaluating could leave political communities open to the kind of self-congratulation about progress that

Forst is worried about with historicists. Additionally, even if we could or have created democratic relationships of power with some institutional supports, they only continue to be democratically justified if the discourses of justification are ongoing for new members.

There is a different, at least as important, challenge when thinking of transtemporal political relationships in a future-oriented way. The idea of political relationships with future people often raises metaphysical questions about the nonexistence (at present) of future beings,[28] but there are other ways of approaching this issue. If politics tracks power, as Forst thinks it does, then we constrain and create spaces of reason for future beings in many intentional and unintentional ways. The question is instead, How can we create contexts of justification with them? What kinds of approaches might we adopt that accord appropriate weight to these political relationships we have now and to those who (we have every reason to expect) will be?

3. OPENNESS AS "MAKING SPACE(S)" FOR NEW CLAIMS OF INJUSTICE

In closing I want to widen my scope back to the broader task I started with—that of identifying strategies in Forst's work that can help fill out what it takes to open political contexts of justice to a wider range of exercises of power and a more inclusive conception of evolving membership. If the task of defining political contexts is itself something that tracks power and if relations of power inevitably shift, then the tools for analyzing the democratic justice of relations of power need to be calibrated to the task of inviting those who are new or unfamiliar.[29] As Forst puts it, the first step in a critical theory of injustice, where we identify unjust relations of power through rule and arbitrary domination, involves the identification of newly visible relations of power between newly entitled members of political communities. With this, newcomers would be seen as having a right to justification of the relations of power, which the political community would rely on in the critique of the injustice of those relations of power. This identification of a being as having a right to justification is already a step toward democratic progress in that it begins to restructure the justifying relationships of power by "counting" the moral standing of newcomers. In many cases, the identification of relations of power could also be a matter of seeing anew the relations of power that rule and dominate members who already have appropriate moral standing in other respects. Progress in identifying one form of domination (say, legal) doesn't preclude also identifying the same persons as dominated through economic relations of power.

There are different challenges in (a) socially integrating wholly new members and (b) socially integrating new aspects or ways of seeing ourselves as related through previously unrecognized forms of political power. In both cases, it's important to consider what conceptual resources they'll/we'll be handed when we endeavor to critique newly identified and recognized relations of injustice. Forst's approaches to greater openness at the level of his theory of political contexts of justice are a model for my own work, in the three ways I identified in the first section. He presses us to adopt wider concepts of the forms of power that should be subject to democratization (openness of political domain), which will in turn involve adjusting our view of political relationships of power to the realities of the exercise of rule, domination, and force (openness of membership). At the level of a critical theory of injustice, he tasks us to work with social sciences in the ongoing process of identifying and prioritizing previously veiled or invisible political relationships (openness as revisability of domain and members).

But I wonder if in starting our critical theoretical tasks with an investigation of political power relationships as he's defined them, we end up presuming more closure to new ways of seeing political power outside the confines of Forstian justification matrices. Doing justice to experiences of injustice requires enormous imagination and creativity and, I think, a disposition to see the unknown *as unknown*. I'm unsure whether fitting experiences of injustice into the conceptual resources of deliberative democracy as defined through Forst's justification theory will be sufficient, precisely because in many subtle ways, his form of deliberative democracy depends on conditions of familiarity and self-knowledge that seem both counterfactual and precisely up for grabs in the contexts of new and evolving membership claims.

I also wonder if attributing to newcomers a right to justification is enough or if it surreptitiously allows us to hem in new theories of injustice by the rule of deliberative democracy and whether that is feasible given the nature of being new—or newly admitted—or appealing for new visibility (or for readmission). I don't have solutions to this challenge, but I want to highlight the importance of asking whether arenas for discourse about justification can be extended to include the permanent reality of political relationships with persons who are unfamiliar to us. It strikes me that there are real limits on the extent to which structures of justification can make space for the constantly evolving new people and new aspects of people that will be politicized as part of our broader emancipatory goals. If we want to avoid the mere look of reciprocity fulfilled instead by proxy arguments on behalf of unknown others, which Forst wants to avoid, then we need to make sense of how social and political norms that span many boundaries can hope to be justified; if in principle that's an impossibility, in the sense of democratic justification, then the arenas of discourse that we work toward should explicitly bear in mind the permanence of contexts of injustice as a corollary of democratic rule.

NOTES

1. Rainer Forst, "Justice, Morality, and Power in the Global Context," in *Real World Justice: Grounds, Principles, Human Rights, and Social Institutions*, ed. Andreas Follesdal and Thomas Pogge (Dordrecht: Springer, 2005), 32.

2. Rainer Forst, "Toward a Critical Theory of Transnational Justice," in *The Right to Justification: Elements of a Constructivist Theory of Justice*, trans. Jeff Flynn (New York: Columbia University Press, 2007), 242–47; Sebastião Salgado, "The Goldmine Portfolio," in *World Poverty and Human Rights*, by Thomas Pogge (Malden, MA: Polity, 2002). The inspiration for this part of Forst's argument comes from an image that appears on the cover of Thomas Pogge's book *World Poverty and Human Rights*.

3. Forst, "Toward a Critical Theory," 247.

4. This alone is complicated and evolving. Revolutions and social movements often center on the expansion of membership status and legal rights to those subjected to laws who were previously voiceless and marginalized.

5. Forst, "The Rules of Reasons: Three Models of Deliberative Democracy," in *Right to Justification*, 155.

6. Rainer Forst, "Transnational Justice and Non-domination: A Discourse-Theoretical Approach," in *Normativity and Power: Analyzing Social Orders of Justification*, trans. Ciaran Cronin (Oxford: Oxford University Press, 2017), 222.
7. Rainer Forst, "Justifying Justification," trans. Ciaran Cronin, in *Justice, Democracy and the Right to Justification: Rainer Forst in Dialogue*, ed. David Owen (New York: Bloomsbury, 2014), 205. See also Forst, "Justifying Justification," 201.

8. Forst, "Transnational Justice and Non-domination," 216. See also Nancy Fraser, "Transnationalizing the Public Sphere," in *Transnationalizing the Public Sphere*, ed. Kate Nash (Cambridge: Polity, 2014), 19.
9. Rainer Forst, "First Things First: Redistribution, Recognition and Justification," *European Journal of Political Theory* 6, no. 3 (2007): 295.
10. Forst, "Toward a Critical Theory," 266.
11. Forst, "First Things First," 295.
12. Forst, "Rule of Reasons," 173. Forst defends this as a recursive answer, "since the norms that have to be justified by reason will turn into reciprocally and generally binding and legally enforced norms, the reasons that confer legitimacy upon them must themselves by reciprocally and generally justifiable."
13. Forst, "Justifying Justification," 201.
14. Ibid.; Eva Ermann, review of *The Right to Justification: Elements of a Constructivist Theory of Justice*, by Rainer Forst, *Notre Dame Philosophical Reviews*, May 24, 2012, http://ndpr.nd.edu/news/the-right-to-justification-elements-of-a-constructivist-theory-of-justice/.
15. Forst, "Critique of Justifying Reason: Explaining Practical Normativity," in *Normativity and Power: Analyzing Social Orders of Justification*, trans. Ciaran Cronin (Oxford: Oxford University Press, 2017), 34.
16. Forst, "Introduction," in *Normativity and Power*, 10.
17. Philip Pettit, *On the People's Terms: A Republican Theory and Model of Democracy* (Cambridge: Cambridge University Press, 2010); Philip Pettit, *Republicanism: A Theory of Freedom and Government* (Oxford: Clarendon, 1997); Philip Pettit, "The Domination Complaint," *Nomos* 86 (2005): 87–117.
18. Forst, *Normativity and Power*, 50.
19. Ibid.
20. William Connolly, "The Complexity of Sovereignty," in *Sovereign Lives: Power in Global Politics*, ed. Jenny Edkins, Veronique Pin-Fat, and Michael J. Shapiro (New York: Routledge, 2004); Patricia Owens, "Accidents Don't Just Happen: The Liberal Politics of High-Technology 'Humanitarian War,'" *Millennium: Journal of International Studies* 32, no. 3 (2003): 595–616; Peter Nyers, "The Accidental Citizen: Acts of Sovereignty and (Un)making Citizenship," *Economy and Society* 35, no. 1 (2006): 22–41. See Connolly, Owens, and Nyers for discussion of "accidental citizenship" in contrast with essential citizenship.
21. Forst, "First Things First," 302.
22. John Rawls, *Justice as Fairness: A Restatement*, ed. Erin Kelly (Cambridge, MA: Belknap, 2001), 8; Susan Moller Okin, *Justice, Gender, and the Family* (New York: Basic Books, 1989), 90–93. This example relates to important criticism Okin advanced against Rawls, which he later aimed to absorb more or less.
23. Forst, "Critique of Justifying Reason: Explaining Practical Normativity," in *Normativity and Power*, 34.

24. Stephen Holmes, "Precommitment and the Paradox of Democracy," in *Passion and Constraints: On the Theory of Liberal Democracy*, ed. John Elster (Chicago: University of Chicago Press, 1995), 134–77; Bonnie Honig, *Emergency Politics: Paradox, Law, Democracy* (Princeton: Princeton University Press, 2009); Jürgen Habermas, "Constitutional Democracy: A Paradoxical Union of Contradictory Principles?," *Political Theory* 29, no. 6 (2001): 766–81.

25. Juan F. Perea, "The Echoes of Slavery: Recognizing the Racist Origins of the Agricultural and Domestic Worker Exclusion from the National Labor Relations Act," *Ohio State Law Journal* 72, no. 1 (2011): 95–138, http://moritzlaw.osu.edu/students/groups/oslj/files/2012/04/72.1.perea_.pdf.

26. I am grateful to American historian Andrew Shankman for his insights on the Twelfth Amendment and the 1911 Apportionment Act in this context.

27. Daria Roithmayr, *How Everyday Choices Lock in White Advantage* (New York: New York University Press, 2014); Maggie Anderson, *Our Black Year: One Family's Quest to Buy Black in America's Racially Divided Economy* (Philadelphia: Perseus Books, 2012). Anderson draws the explicit connection between lynching and long-term economic domination, while Roithmayr provides parallel arguments about what I'm calling transtemporal racial injustice.

28. Within population ethics, philosophers have worried about how we can justify obligations to future generations in terms of the so-called nonidentity problem. While I don't have space to develop it here, I think there are useful connections being drawn by environmental ethicists in this context.

29. Forst, "Introduction," in *Normativity and Power*, 8.

CHAPTER 8

A Feminist Engagement with Forst's Transnational Justice

Sarah Clark Miller

1. INTRODUCTION

This chapter offers a feminist engagement with and evaluation of Rainer Forst's concept of transnational justice, especially as he articulates it in his most recent book, *Normativity and Power: Analyzing Social Orders of Justification.*[1] While focusing on this book, the analysis I offer also builds on his earlier writings on a critical theory of transnational justice and the concept of the right to justification. Feminist theoretical resources, including current transnational feminist theory, provide a series of lenses that bring into focus the strengths and weaknesses of Forst's approach. This is particularly true with regard to the issue of whether he offers a theory of transnational justice sensitive to the gendered dimensions of global injustice, as well as to the realities of a nonideal world. At key moments in the paper, I draw on examples of transnational gender-based and sexual violence as representative of a specific and prolific form of gendered global injustice to illustrate my argument. The argument advances in two main steps. First, I consider ways in which Forst's work is feminist in nature and explore how he might reinforce feminist theoretical efforts. I then identify limitations of Forst's theory from a transnational feminist perspective, exploring how feminist philosophers might challenge aspects of his approach. In this vein, I offer reflections relating to two main concepts: the tensions between ideal and nonideal theory within Forst's work and the idea of adaptive preferences.

One main evaluative bar I employ is whether any given theory of global justice has the resources to properly perceive and suggest a response to the specifically gendered dimensions of global injustice. The significance of this mode of evaluation is based on the contention that proper attention and response to forms of structural oppression are indispensable elements of any adequate theory of transnational justice. In order to investigate this point concretely, I delve into a global issue that, although widespread, has received scant attention in the global justice literature. This is the problem of transnational sexual violence. Recognition of potential limitations in Forst's work and elsewhere in the broader global justice literature in this regard serves as an opportunity to transform discourses of global justice—for example, by highlighting the importance of concepts such as interdependence, power, and vulnerability instead of more standard concepts such as independence, autonomy, and universalism. Regarding transnational sexual violence specifically, we must conceptualize transnational sexual violence as a social and political fact arising from necessarily complex histories, rather than as "natural" or representative of how some cultures treat "their" women. Approaching transnational sexual violence from a perspective of ideal theory and largely acontextually results in analyses that are deeply flawed and, in fact, that can perpetrate additional forms of harm.

Gaining an empirical sense of the magnitude of the problem represents a good place to start. How many people worldwide are victims/survivors[2] of sexual violence? Though this question is fairly straightforward, answering it is unfortunately anything but. If we flip the terms of this question, calling attention to the so-often occluded role of perpetrators by asking how many people worldwide perpetrate sexual violence, answers become murkier still. While the reasons for the opacity of both questions are crucially important—including elements such as the many disincentives victims/survivors have to report violations and culturally disparate notions of what counts as sexual violence—proper exploration of such reasons would require extensive space not available here and will not be my primary focus. I will therefore only construct an estimate of the scope of incidents of sexual violence worldwide, one that necessarily carries with it some serious limitations.

According to the World Health Organization (WHO), more than one in three women experience "physical and/or sexual intimate partner violence or non-partner sexual violence in their lifetime."[3] The WHO estimates this to be true for 35 percent of the female population worldwide, which is approximately 17.3 percent of the overall human population. We can therefore estimate that globally, approximately 1.3 billion women are the victims/survivors of physical and/or sexual intimate-partner violence or nonpartner sexual violence.[4] What some might find surprising is that the magnitude of these numbers rivals that of two other contemporary moral problems that receive a much greater share of attention in the global justice literature—namely, global hunger and poverty. Approximately 795 million people,[5] or 10.6 percent of the human population, are undernourished, and 767 million people,[6] or 10.2 percent of the human population, exist in conditions of extreme poverty, here understood as living on less than $1.90 a day. All three of these contemporary moral issues are dire, to say the least. I want to suggest a momentary comparative analysis of them not in order to demonstrate that one issue is necessarily worse than the other. Rather, I do so to establish that the underappreciated global moral problem of transnational sexual violence is similar in magnitude and nature of harm to the much more frequently and thoroughly discussed global injustices of hunger and poverty.

Comparative analysis shows that the prevalence of the sexual assault of women (including rape) is 6.7 percent higher than the prevalence of undernourished people and 7.1 percent higher than the number of people living in extreme poverty. We must also keep in mind that the transnational sexual-violence statistic likely does not encapsulate the full extent of the matter both because of its exclusion of men and gender-nonconforming populations and because it does not record the repeated instances of physical and/or sexual intimate-partner and/or nonpartner sexual violence to which many women are subjected. Even so, transnational sexual violence clearly represents the greatest magnitude of the three global problems.[7]

Demonstrating that transnational sexual violence has a similar (and even slightly greater) magnitude than the more frequently explored issues of global justice or hunger and poverty justifies considering this issue alongside other major contemporary moral problems of a global scope. Moreover, taking the underexplored issue of transnational sexual violence as our starting point for an examination of global or transnational justice makes plain the ways in which aspects of the global justice literature are often insensitive to gendered dimensions of transnational injustice and therefore inadequate from a feminist theoretical standpoint. Transnational sexual violence quickly pushes the global justice discourse to its conceptual limits.

Forst's theory, however, goes some distance toward addressing this problem. Some of the ways in which he is critical of the global justice discourse, most recently in *Normativity and Power*, map directly onto and support feminist critiques of the same. Beyond critical engagement with the philosophical literature, there are promising synergies between Forst's positive theory and some global and transnational feminist theories, as I will detail in the next section. Any theory that has the resources to address transnational sexual violence must evidence a strong attunement to and consideration of remedies for structural domination and injustice. Forst makes great strides along this path. But that same path also contains stumbling blocks that can be difficult to navigate. These include the challenges inherent in a split theory, one half of which appears to be fully ideal and features a foundational notion of justification that exists beyond immanent critique, as I will discuss in the third section.

To be clear, my overarching point is not to demonstrate that Forst's work fails as a theory of transnational sexual violence—a task that was never his to begin with. Instead, it is to note that inasmuch as we believe that a theory of transnational justice must be able to identify and address the specifically gendered dimensions of such injustice, Forst's theory succeeds in some regards and requires further development in others. What is most important, however, is how the exercise of identifying both the strengths and weaknesses of his theory leads us to a better understanding of what might compose a philosophically and practically successful theory of transnational justice—one that furnishes us with the means to perceive, engage, and respond to widespread patterns and varied representations of transnational injustice.

2. POINTS OF SYNERGY AND OPPORTUNITIES FOR EXPANSION

There are multiple aspects of Forst's philosophy that are feminist in nature, which I take to be an important strength of his work. For example, Forst's approach to justification and normativity can augment and sharpen global and transnational feminist work on self-reflexive critique. And feminist philosophers can, for instance, synergistically endorse and further Forst's insistence in *Normativity and Power* on the importance of engaging "intersubjective relations and social structures" rather than "subjective or supposedly objective states of the provision of goods."[8] At the heart of Forst's work rests a methodology of critique, a feature that is, of course, shared by many critical theorists. In *Normativity and Power*, Forst sets himself apart from a perhaps more standard way of engaging critique in critical theory— that is, a strictly immanent one—in order to show the vital role that transcendental critique might play as well. His focus is on justification as a method that can generate critique, as well as on justification as a moral foundation.

The methodology of critique is shared by some feminist philosophers working on globalization and, more specifically, occupies the heart of transnational feminist theory. Emphasis on the importance of critique also serves to distinguish transnational feminist theory from international or global feminist theory. For the transnational feminist, one goal is a consistent engagement with the content of feminist claims made in order to detect any privileging of dominant views and exclusion of nondominant views. This move resonates strongly through much of Forst's corpus on justification and represents a place of significant synergy between Forst's approach and feminist approaches. In fact, in *Normativity and Power*, Forst offers an important advance on which feminists may well wish to draw. (I will return to this point later.)

Let me first provide an example designed to illustrate how critique works in transnational feminist philosophy in order to establish modes of connection with Forst's philosophy. Consider two very different contexts in which sexual violence takes place: campus sexual assault in North America and rape used as a weapon of war in the conflict (and now slow recovery from conflict) in the Democratic Republic of Congo. Dissimilarities between these two circumstances are immediately apparent. The economic, geopolitical, and material contexts (among others) diverge significantly. Nevertheless, in both settings, there is a relatively high incidence of sexual violence. What, if anything, are we to make of this commonality? What might the nature of its ethical or political significance be?

Considering a more specific example of sexual violence from each context may help further focus this line of questioning. When a fraternity member rapes a female undergraduate at a fraternity party on a university campus in the United States,[9] what relationship, if any, does this event have with a second instance of sexual violence in which a soldier rapes a woman in South Kivu in the Democratic Republic of Congo as she returns from a river where she was fetching water?[10] Are these two events completely separate? Related in some particular way? Are the American and Congolese women who experience them connected in some significant way? Might there be something troubling about comparing their experiences in the first place, given the considerable differences in structural positionality they occupy, as well as the possible social power that they have at their disposal? How can we best conceptualize the nature of the ethical and/or political relationship between these two cases?

Within feminist theory, different camps would provide rather significantly contrasting answers to these questions—and most importantly, with differing methodologies and levels of critical apparatus in play. Here I will focus specifically on global or international feminist responses to these questions versus transnational feminist responses. I emphasize the tensions between these two camps of feminist theory because those tensions highlight the synergies between transnational feminist work and Forst's philosophy, specifically with regard to methodologies of critique.

In thinking through the meaning of transnational sexual violence and the nature of possible ethical or political connection between specific, differently situated cases, global feminists would assert the commonality of gender oppression that ties these two cases and women together. Global feminism represents a dominant strand of thought originating in second-wave feminism. From their perspective, patriarchy is a global institution and is universal in scope. As a result, both the American woman and the Congolese woman suffer similarly at the hands of patriarchy when they are assaulted sexually. In one significant respect, their plights are essentially the same. Ethical and political resonance exists between the examples from the United States and the Democratic Republic of Congo, opening up a space for connections of solidarity between women from very different cultures. While the focus on solidarity between women that global feminism fosters is valuable, the essentialism of supposed shared life or social experiences that ultimately grounds that solidarity and concepts like "global sisterhood"[11] is deeply problematic.

This is where the feminist approach to critique enters the picture. Transnational feminists would rightly note that harm results from the way in which global feminists tamp down the ethically and politically significant differences between the American and the Congolese women in the example. Transnational feminists charge global feminists with insensitivity and ignorance rising from how their methodological approach rests on a false universal of sorts and on implicit claims that their experience (i.e., the experience of relatively privileged, mostly white Western feminists) represents the experiences of all. A proper mode of critique underscores how their experiences are far from even being generalizable. Transnational feminists would not deny that there is a prevalence of male perpetration of sexual assault against female victims worldwide. Understanding the nature of this prevalence, however, need not resort to gender essentialism and the citing of shared experiences where none exist. Beyond the insulting elision of difference that a global feminist approach may entail, such a framework can, in fact, homogenize the ethically and politically significant differences that exist between women's struggles for gender justice and that most need to be seen to avoid an automatic prioritizing of the social justice interests of women from the Global North.[12]

131

It is because of the ways in which transnational feminists are avowedly, self-reflexively critical that they can uncover the false universals that compose a serious portion of global feminisms. This is emblematic of the important function that critique plays within the context of feminist philosophy and echoes, I believe, the work that Forst's concept of justification can do. The participant-focused perspective, which is part and parcel of Forst's groundbreaking contribution of a remaking of the Kantian notion of basic respect for autonomy as the right to justification, goes some way toward challenging false universals. Critique in this mode is intended by feminists as immanent critique, designed to uncover and emend Western feminist values (e.g., "Sisterhood is Global!") that homogenize difference while masquerading as universal. Transnational feminisms and, in a related vein, I believe, Forst's approach, can offer an alternative, more successful approach to and framing of transnational sexual violence. (Forst's notion of justification does, of course, draw upon more than only the immanent, with a significant role for the transcendental too. This marks a point of difference from strictly immanent forms of critique found in some veins of feminist philosophy.) In a transnational feminist framework, female victims/survivors of sexual violence need not be seen as all sharing some core experience. The very real material, social, and ideological differences between women are not smoothed over or ignored in the name of promoting solidarity among women against an overarching system of patriarchy. For transnational feminist theorists, the impetus of solidarity is political rather than metaphysical. Women need not share any core experience in order to back one another's shared political or social interests. They need not claim a tightly knit sisterhood in order to be politically committed to one another and to a process of resisting and overcoming the realities of transnational sexual violence.

As the explicitly political foundation of transnational feminism comes into view, so too does a possible difference with Forst, as well as an opportunity for reconsidering the role of critique within transnational feminism by thinking about aspects of *Normativity and Power*. In this text, Forst offers what I view as an important challenge to the position that critique must necessarily be entirely immanent. He reminds us that "the fact that a critique is immanent is neither a reason for nor a hallmark of its legitimacy."[13] I have come to think of this as a challenge to what sometimes seems like the fetishization or overvaluation of the immanent that can be found in some feminist approaches to ethical and political thought. Forst issues this challenge through the concept of radical critique. He writes,

> Who would want to suggest to a critic of the Indian caste system who rejects this system in toto that she should please proceed in an "immanent" way? Or remind a critic of patriarchy in a given society in which this was hardly ever challenged that she should not speak a "foreign language"? Would that not amount to ostracizing such critics from social discourses? Those who understand criticism as an autonomous practice of challenging existing orders of justification will not formulate an artificial opposition between internal or immanent criticism, on the one hand, and external criticism, on the other. Rather, they will orient themselves exclusively to the quality of the social analysis and the demand for reciprocity and generality, even where this is "unheard of" and goes far beyond the firmly established understandings of justifiability or ethical life. Radical criticism may be immanent or transcending so that it is no longer clear where the one form of criticism ends and the other begins. . . . Settled ethical life is the object of criticism, not its ground or limit. Critical theory cannot dispense with the transcending power of reason, which may venture into regions that were previously unthinkable.[14]

I want first to draw from this quote what I think is most insightful for feminist theorists and then switch gears to question the implications of one part of it for the rest of Forst's theory. Forst notes that preconceptions about proper modes of critique, ones that expect an exclusive reliance on immanent sources and draw lines regarding which forms of critical engagement are best, can stymie efforts at social emancipation on the part of agents internal to repressive cultures. Thinking again in terms of transnational sexual violence, we can map Forst's concerns onto a context in which women, living in a non-Western culture that does not recognize marital rape—as was true in the United States until 1993, when marital rape exemptions were finally withdrawn in all states—publically object to the practice by citing bodily integrity as a human right. If such women were to be questioned for incorporating a supposedly external, Western value of human rights, it would be, to my mind, fair and correct to object to this judgment. Such a position of so objecting belies ignorance because there is a convincing case to be made that there is nothing inherently Western about the concept of human rights (as well as the concept of bodily integrity). Moreover, even if they were values rooted in the West that had migrated to a non-Western culture, where women seeking emancipation found them useful, why shouldn't they use those concepts? In these ways, I agree with Forst. This kind of example, as well as the one Forst includes in the quote earlier, serves as a reminder that a sanctimonious approach to a critical method can itself be a force of domination. This reminder is an important one. The means of emancipation from forms of domination should not be limited by a predetermined sense of the importance of the immanent.

But I also want to point out something quite important about this discussion of repressive uses of the prevalence of the imma-nent. The context for the suspicion regarding the transcendental that caused feminists to return to the immanent is utterly crucial to foreground here. It wasn't because of some desire to erect new rules of critique that feminists doing emancipatory work in the world turned to the immanent, the local, and the contextual. And it wasn't because they blindly focused on the immanent to the exclu-sion of the transcendental. The turn toward the immanent, the local, the situated, and the contextual happened for at least two reasons. One of these reasons was because of centuries of a different mode in which multiple concepts said to be universal and human were in fact culturally coded as masculine and white and were therefore less open to those who weren't those things (male and white) and were therefore thought to be less true of lesser humans—for example, women, persons of color, and the disabled. The move to immanence occurred because of centuries of very damaging, exceedingly hegemonic deployment of supposedly transcendentally grounded notions that somehow still bore the marks of domination. Sure, women could reason, but not as well as men. Recall Kant's quote about the abilities of scholarly women: "As concerns scholarly women: they use their *books* somewhat like their *watch,* that is, they carry one so that it will be seen that they have one; though it is usually not running or not set by the sun."[15] The other reason for the emphasis on and valorization of the immanent was a much-needed and late-arriving awareness on the part of predominantly white feminists from the Global North of the ways in which their forms of feminism were actually forms of imperialist feminism in which they placed their values, narratives, and experiences at the center of the discourse, thereby marginalizing and sometimes completely erasing the values, narratives, and experiences of women of color. With regard to sexual violence in particular, such narratives implicitly locate the Global North as a bastion of empowerment, a place of less sexual oppression than "other" locations, such as, say, the entirety of the Global South. Gender empowerment, in a purely self-congratulatory fashion, given who proclaims such views, is presented as widespread throughout the Global North. Moreover, because of their relatively empowered position, those in the Global North (read: socioeconomically stable, often white) are to "save" homogenized masses of brown women existing in conditions of relative material scarcity. As you can see, imperial feminism is also guilty of generalizing other cultures and of failing to apply intersectional analyses appropriately sensitive to the intricate dynamics of domination that may well be present.

Thus turning to the local and the immanent is notably a morally and politically vital process of decentering the hegemonic Western view or the view of the Global North in order to open up space for proper weight and credibility to be given to situated epistemologies and local understandings. So while I appreciate Forst's movement against unthinkingly endorsing immanent critique, there may, in fact, be important historical reasons to appreciate its inclusion. Forst would likely be amenable to this position.

3. LIMITATIONS AND QUESTIONS

a. *The Ideal and the Nonideal*

136   I have just argued that what ultimately motivated the turn toward the immanent was the recognition that forms of supposedly universal values when espoused either by white feminists from the Global North or by white male philosophers were anything but. They were, instead, immanent, local, situated beliefs masquerading as transcendental ones. That is the core of the concern here. Holding that firmly in mind matters quite a bit when assessing charges that some theorists go overboard in challenging the possibility of universal discourses while holding tight to the moral importance of local, immanent critique.

    Let me articulate the concern I am raising another way and through a different framework—namely, as a shift from ideal theory to non-ideal theory. Social theory that draws on the immanent is nonideal theory, while social theory grounded in the transcendental serves as an example of ideal theory. Theories like Forst's draw on both. The split between the ideal and the nonideal that exists internal to Forst's own system provides an interesting lens through which to analyze the extended quote from Forst that I considered in the last section. There Forst argues powerfully that radical critique stemming from external criticism is not only legitimately possible but also deeply desirable. Importantly, there is a major matter to settle here. It is a line of tension within Forst's theory that appears to serve as the source of multiple, related forms of criticism of that work. And it is a distinction that Forst ultimately seems to complicate. Part of this argument rests on a notable moment of blurring for Forst that I think is justified but that also appears to possibly create some serious difficulties for him. This is the moment where he notes that "radical criticism may be immanent or transcending so that it is no longer clear where the one form of criticism ends and the other begins."[16] Yet this sense of not knowing where one form of criticism ends and the other begins creates problems for a theory based on the distinction between the ideal foundations on which it rests and the nonideal mode of social criticism that is its content. Another way of articulating this is as a split between mutually owed justification as a concept that grounds the moral authority of Forst's system in the transcendental and justification as a mode of immanent social critique with the power to detect and shift patterns of social domination. Much of Forst's system is based on this very split and, in fact, tension between the transcendental and the immanent. He, in fact, requires this split in order to attain what I take are several main objectives in his theory.

Most importantly, Forst turns to the ideal to establish an incontrovertible foundation for the moral authority of a requirement for a certain form of intersubjective engagement, one in which we are called to give reasons to one another and, notably, to those who are less well situated than ourselves in terms of societal patterns of oppression. This aim is vital, as the risk of relativism is real. A theory that renders a contextualism of nondomination just one variety of contextualism competing among many other seemingly desirable others is not the outcome we want. And yet, a criticism waits in the wings. Lois McNay characterizes the problem this way: "Forst's attempt to transcendentalise the justification principle replicates the ideological errors of ideal theory where contingent social practices are reified as free-floating universal norms."[17] I want to explore further the nature of the complaint raised against Forst regarding the ideal nature of the right to justification. I take McNay's and other's concerns to be based on a standard objection against ideal theory, which Charles Mills names as ideal theory's "reliance on idealization to the exclusion, or at least marginalization, of the actual."[18] Does the move to the transcendental, to the ideal, necessarily block the self-scrutiny required to guard against the vices of ideal theory? In order to address this issue, don't we need something that can critique critique? Otherwise, how do we guard against at least two of the vices of ideal theory that Mills discusses that seem most pertinent here—namely, the second vice of idealized capacities including perfect rationality and agential abilities and the fifth vice of an idealized cognitive sphere that does not register the impact of developing and living in conditions of structural injustice?

McNay elaborates on these concerns in a slightly different fashion: "Put bluntly, how exhaustive can critique's reflection upon its own presumptions, blind-spots and potential exclusions be if its animating core supposedly floats free of particular configurations of power?"[19] And yet the actual does not make a sound foundation for a universal, binding ethic. So what is Forst to do? What Forst seeks to avoid in grounding justification in this way is the possibility of relativism and arbitrariness. What happens instead is a form of idealization that renders that foundation theoretically suspect.

Forst is in a tough position here. McNay captures the nature of the bind well:

> In the end, Forst's vacillation is perhaps inevitable in so far as his goals of establishing independent moral grounds for critique, on the one side, and of developing a penetrating critical theory of injustice, on the other, have greater contradictory entailments for political reasoning than he is prepared to acknowledge. In so far as they cannot be reconciled, they represent what Adorno calls torn halves which, when brought together, do not add up to a unified whole. . . . A solution to Forst's difficulties, given his stated allegiance to Frankfurt school critique, would be to let go of the transcendental side of his project and construe the right to justification as a contingent historical achievement albeit one that is akin to what other critical theorists term an immanent universal. Historicising justification in this manner would enhance reflexive elaboration of the concept although it would undoubtedly mean giving up on a certain type of strong universalism.[20]

If critique's normative grounding comes from something imbued with particular configurations of power, then it would not be universal and, more important, would not provide a rock-solid normative basis. If critique accepts these immanent foundations, it loses its fundamental moral authority and enters the very real risk of relativism. Yet if critique doesn't acknowledge that we have no unmediated access to the transcendental—that it is always necessarily mediated by our situatedness, our immanence—it runs the risk of continuing a long history of articulating a false universal.

McNay indicates that one way forward involves the immanent universal and suggests that Forst need not fear detranscendentalizing the governing principle of his system as much as he does. She feels that such detranscendentalizing would not rob critique of "the capacity for systematic social criticism and generalizable normative relevance."[21] But my guess is that the *immanent universal* that McNay suggests is a far cry from Forst's notion of an *enlightened universal*. Given what Forst has said about enlightened particularism not being the solution to the problem of happy parochialism, with enlightened universalism instead being the only answer, I suspect that the way through for Forst rests in the concept of the enlightened universal.[22]

b. Global Gender Injustice, Intrasubjective Justification, and Adaptive Preferences

Having pressed the issue of how Forst might navigate the Scylla of relativism and the Charybdis of vices of ideal theory, I would like to return to and focus directly on transnational justice and gender injustice first by sustaining attention on chapter 10 of *Normativity and Power*, entitled "Transnational Justice and Non-domination: A Discourse-Theoretical Approach."

Moments where Forst's approach and transnational feminist theory overlap and reinforce one another are plentiful. For example, transnational feminists would concur with Forst when he asserts that "in order to do justice to those who suffer from injustice, one must grasp the relational and structural dimension of justice and liberate oneself from an understanding that is focused exclusively on quantities of goods. Justice must be directed to intersubjective relations and social structure, not to subjective or supposedly objective states of the provision of goods."[23] Interrelational and structural approaches are necessary for producing accounts attuned to the complex movements of power, and Forst's work is indispensable in this regard. Transnational feminist theorists would also find themselves in hearty agreement with the critique Forst issues when he notes the shortcomings of goods-based or strictly individual well-being-based accounts of global justice for the ways in which such approaches fail to appreciate, as he writes, that "justice is a matter of *who determines who receives what* and not only or primarily of who should receive what."[24] This move highlights the importance of incorporating a participant-focused perspective, while not solely resting there: the analysis of why and how participants receive what they do is equally important.

Building on what Forst provides, we can add a friendly amendment that moves beyond his call for an awareness of "who determines who receives what" now to a broader awareness of historical patterns of injustice and coloniality that result in an unequal distribution of wealth, for example. Thus transnational justice is not only a matter of who determines and receives what in the contemporary moment. Feminist theorists of both postcolonial and transnational stripes rightfully demand more attention to the history of coloniality involved.

In addition, drawing on Forst's earlier writing, Amy Allen notes that Forst has argued that "a critical theory of transnational justice must conceptualize what he calls the fact of multiple domination, for those who are dominated, particularly in the developing world, are most often 'dominated by their own (hardly legitimate) governments, elites, or warlords, which in turn are both working together and are (at least partly) dominated by global actors. Especially women and children are the subjects of even further relations of domination within the family and local community.'"[25]

I take it that a theory of multiple domination maps onto a theory of intersectionality and could, then, identify ways in which there is an amplification of domination where there are intersecting lines of identity. We cannot make progress in thinking about justice beyond the state unless we develop a realistic and critical view of the many and complex relations of domination within, between, and beyond the states that mark our global predicament.

Yet when it comes to global gender injustice, an issue that feminist theorists have long grappled with proves equally, if differently, challenging for Forst. I refer here to the concept of adaptive preferences, which proves to be a problem for Forst specifically in relation to not *inter*subjective justification but rather *intra*subjective justification. Feminist philosophers understand adaptive preferences as referring to preferences (or desires or interests) women hold that are formed by and function in service of forms of oppression in which those women exist. Adaptive preferences can function as a barrier to liberation: if one makes decisions and acts in ways that sustain the conditions of one's own oppression, freedom from oppression will likely be much more difficult—if not impossible—to attain. Feminists have developed multiple, competing theories of adaptive preferences.[26] We need not review the finer details of these important debates here in order to understand a key problem that adaptive preferences present to Forst's theory.

To fully understand the nature of the difficulty, consider again two cases of sexual violence. The first is the case of a female student at a large university in the United States whom another student gets very intoxicated and then has sex with when she is so inebriated that she is not able to give meaningful consent. She does not see this as rape, even though legally it is considered so. It is, at best, a case of extremely unjust sex. She refuses to consider it as such. The second case is of another woman in the United States who, according to religious doctrine, believes herself to be subservient to her husband and necessarily available for his sexual advances even when she does not wish to so engage. In the context of marriage, it does not even occur to her that she has a right to consent or not. She engages many times in sex when it is expressly against her desires and when she does not consent to it. She in no way sees this as a violation, let alone as a case of marital rape.

What are we to say about situations such as these in which victims/survivors of sexual violence accept and sometimes even feel they prefer the circumstances of their own oppression? When you attempt to give those evidencing adaptive preferences—such as the two victims/survivors in the prior cases—reasons for why the form of treatment they are receiving is detrimental to them, fails to regard them as moral equals, violates their autonomy, or does not contribute to their flourishing, they do not want to hear what you are saying and do not want to believe you. They are complicit in their own oppression. In fact, beyond being complicit, they seek it and may even desire it (as an example of what are sometimes called "deformed desires"). In addition to being subject to oppressive conditions, they also oppress themselves. Although it may first seem strange, this appears to be a case of intrapersonal domination.

To frame this nexus of problems in a way specifically relevant to Forst's theory, we might ask, How does the right to justification treat such cases? Does it have the resources to do so? Forst writes, "True alienation consists in not seeing oneself and others as socially, morally, and politically autonomous subjects of justification or as authorities within a normative order."[27] In line with this quote, it appears that adaptive preference is a form of alienation. The key question, therefore, to ask is this: How might Forst respond to those who in some meaningful way wish to reject or forfeit the basic right to justification? Does Forst's account have resources to respond meaningfully to this type of phenomenon?

I fear that it does not. Those who would reject or forfeit the basic right to justification in this case are not seeking emancipation—in fact, quite the opposite. Forst writes, "The primary victim of injustice is not the person who lacks certain goods but instead the person who does not 'count' in the production and allocation of goods."[28] What do we do about those who feel that it is right that they not count? They are not particularly self-determining and do not wish to be so. In short, what does this theory have to say about cases where we are complicit in our own oppression? Do we have an obligation to resist?

4. CONCLUSION

My efforts have been to bring a balanced perspective—both appreciative and critical—to aspects of Rainer Forst's work primarily from a transnational feminist perspective. A theory that is at moments feminist in its own right, Forst's work provides rich resources for synergistic interaction with and furthering of the project of a theory of transnational justice attuned to the realities of global gender injustice. Transnational sexual violence has been the primary instance of global gender injustice that I have considered. I have also identified what I take to be some limitations of the work from a feminist and nonideal theory perspective. Overall, the synergies between Forst and feminist philosophical work strike me as promising and warrant additional exploration of how together the two philosophical approaches might provide interwoven responses to transnational injustice.

NOTES

1. Rainer Forst, *Normativity and Power: Analyzing Social Orders of Justification*, trans. Ciaran Cronin (New York: Oxford University Press, 2017).

2. I have chosen to use the term *victim/survivor* in this chapter in recognition of the fact that the terms *victim* and *survivor* alone do not adequately represent the complex identity or self-understanding that those who have experienced sexual violence can hold. The term *victim/survivor* attempts to acknowledge the range of possible self-conceptualization that might follow the experience of sexual violence.

3. "Violence Against Women," World Health Organization, accessed August 4, 2017, http://www.who.int/mediacentre/factsheets/fs239/en/; "Global and Regional Estimates of Violence Against Women: Prevalence and Health Effects of Intimate Partner Violence and Non-partner Sexual Violence," World Health Organization, accessed August 4, 2017, https://www.who.int/reproductivehealth/publications/violence/9789241564625/en/.

4. As of September 2017, the world population is approximately 7.5 billion (see "Current World Population," Worldometers, accessed September 1, 2017, http://www.worldometers.info/world-population/); 49.55 percent of the world population is female (see "Population, Female [% of Total]," World Bank, accessed September 1, 2017, https://data.worldbank.org/indicator/SP.POP.TOTL.FE.ZS); 7.53 billion people × 49.55 percent female population = 3.73 billion women in the world. Using the WHO estimate of a violation rate of 35 percent, I have calculated that 1.30 billion women, which represents 17.3 percent of the overall human population, are victims of physical and/or sexual intimate partner violence or nonpartner sexual violence. I recognize that I am including the part of the female world population who are children. My guess is that rates of childhood sexual violence against female children are higher than rates of sexual violence against adults, which would likely render my estimate even higher than it already is. Childhood sexual assault, however, is not the focus of this particular chapter.

5. "Global Hunger Relief Statistics," Global Hunger Relief, accessed September 1, 2017, http://globalhungerrelief.com/statistics.

6. World Bank, *Poverty and Shared Prosperity 2016: Taking on Inequality*, accessed September 1, 2017, http://www.worldbank.org/en/publication/poverty-and-shared-prosperity.

7. I do not have the space here to address the forms of interaction among the three contemporary moral problems I am considering but do want to note that understanding the ways in which they may or may not be codetermining and compounding is important.

8. Forst, *Normativity and Power*, 201.

9. Jennifer L. Truman and Lynn Langton, *Criminal Victimization* (Washington, DC: Bureau of Justice Statistics, 2015), http://www.bjs.gov/index.cfm?ty=pbdetail&iid=5366. See also "Campus Sexual Violence: Statistics," Rape, Abuse & Incest National Network, accessed September 1, 2017, https://www.rainn.org/statistics/campus-sexual-violence.

10. Human Rights Watch, *Soldiers Who Rape, Commanders Who Condone: Sexual Violence and Military Reform in the Democratic Republic of Congo* (New York: Human Rights Watch, 2009); see also Carly Brown, "Rape as a Weapon of War in the Democratic Republic of Congo," *Torture* 22, no. 1 (2012): 24–27.

11. Robin Morgan, ed., *Sisterhood Is Global: The International Women's Movement Anthology* (New York: Feminist Press at CUNY, 1996).

12. Richa Nagar and Amanda Lock Swarr, *Critical Transnational Feminist Praxis* (Albany: SUNY Press, 2010), 4.

13. Forst, *Normativity and Power*, 13.

14. Ibid.

15. Immanuel Kant, *Anthropology from a Pragmatic Point of View*, trans. Robert B. Louden (Cambridge: Cambridge University Press, 2009), 209 (italics in the original).

16. Forst, *Normativity and Power*, 13.

17. Lois McNay, "The Limits of Justification: Critique, Disclosure and Reflexivity," *European Journal of Political Theory* (October 2016): 5, https://journals-sagepub -com.ezaccess.libraries.psu.edu/doi/pdf/10.1177/1474885116670294 (online only).

18. Mills, "'Ideal Theory' as Ideology," *Hypatia* 20, no. 3 (2005): 168.

19. McNay, "Limits of Justification," 7.

20. Ibid., 18.

21. Ibid.

22. Rainer Forst, "The Justification of Progress and the Progress of Justification," this volume.

23. Forst, *Normativity and Power*, 201.

24. Ibid., 202 (italics in the original).

25. Amy Allen, "Power and the Politics of Difference: Oppression, Empowerment, and Transnational Justice," *Hypatia* 23, no. 3 (2008): 170. Allen is quoting from Rainer Forst, "Towards a Critical Theory of Transnational Justice," *Metaphilosophy* 32, nos. 1–2 (2001): 166.

26. Some examples include Martha Nussbaum, "Adaptive Preferences and Women's Options," *Economics and Philosophy* 17 (2001): 67–88; Serene J. Khader, *Adaptive Preferences and Women's Empowerment* (New York: Oxford University Press, 2011); and Natalie Stoljar, "Autonomy and Adaptive Preference Formation," in *Autonomy, Oppression, and Gender*, ed. Andrea Veltman and Mark Piper (New York: Oxford University Press, 2014), 227–52.

27. Forst, *Normativity and Power*, 22.

28. Ibid., 202–3.

144

CHAPTER 9

Progress, Normativity, and Universality

Reply to Forst

Amy Allen

The question of progress has been central to the project of critical theory from the start. Skepticism about reading the history of European modernity as a story of progress runs arguably as deep in the work of Walter Benjamin, Theodor Adorno, and even, after a certain point, Max Horkheimer as does the attempt to redeem some version of this story in Jürgen Habermas's communicative turn. Indeed, although such a reading would be admittedly partial, it would not be wholly misleading to write the history of Habermas's break with the methodology of first-generation critical theory in terms of their radically opposed understandings of progress. According to that version of the story, Habermas is, as he once insisted, the last Marxist standing in the Frankfurt School camp, in the sense that he holds on to the historical materialist view that our hope for progress in the future, in order to count as genuine hope, must be grounded in the objective tendencies of the present, which is to say on some account of historical progress. However nonmetaphysical, pragmatic, and deflationary that account of progress is for Habermas, this position stands in stark contrast to Benjamin and Adorno's straightforward rejection of this tenet of historical materialism. As Adorno put it, with characteristic bluntness, "There is no basis for hope in the objective historical trend."[1] And yet Adorno, at least (if not Benjamin), holds on to the possibility of progress in the future.

146   This deep divide over the concept of progress is not only internal to the project of Frankfurt School critical theory; it also separates much work in post-Habermasian critical theory from a variety of critical theories in the broader sense of that term. In this broader sense, the term *critical theory* might refer to any politically inflected form of cultural, social, or political theory that has critical, progressive, or emancipatory aims, including much work done in the fields of feminist theory, queer theory, critical philosophy of race, and post- and decolonial theory. In these fields, a deep skepticism about progressive philosophies of history—and about foundationalist normative projects more generally—reigns supreme. In large part, the aim of my recent work on progress and normativity was to open up a dialogue between Frankfurt School critical theory and these other strands of critical theory by drawing on both the trenchant critique of progress and the antifoundationalist conception of normativity that can be found in the early Frankfurt School, particularly the work of Adorno.

This broader historical and theoretical background helps situate the present exchange between Rainer Forst and myself. To a large extent, this debate could be understood as a family quarrel—a disagreement about how best to inherit the legacy of Frankfurt School critical theory, carried out between two theorists who take themselves to be committed to this project—but it is one that has broader implications as well: for how this approach to critical theory situates itself with respect to other critical perspectives and for how critical theory might best respond to our "post-" colonial condition. To be sure, to say that this is a family quarrel is not to minimize the degree of conflict involved. As we all know, family quarrels are often the most intense and the most painful, precisely because family members know each other so well.

Despite the fact that we deeply disagree in our understandings of normativity, there are also substantial points of agreement between Forst and myself concerning the concept of progress, and it seems important to begin by elaborating these. First, Forst and I agree about the dialectical nature of the concept of progress, which he characterizes as a "tension between its normative and its historical meaning" (see chapter 2, 18). I attempt to capture something similar with my distinction between progress as a "fact"—that is, the historical claim that there has been progress up to now, a claim that is both empirical and normative—and progress as an imperative, which is the normative claim that some development or other would count as making things better, more just, or less oppressive. We further agree that the historical meaning of progress has up to now been entangled with ideologically imperialist and neocolonial assumptions. Second, however, we also agree that there is an important sense in which even the radical postcolonial critique of progress depends on some understanding of progress. In other words, to borrow once again Forst's pithy formulation, one can't be against progress without in some sense being for it. If I critique the ideologically imperialist and neocolonial misuses to which the concept of historical progress has been put, then I am at least implicitly committed to saying that it would be better if we could rid ourselves of this ideology—thus to some sense of what would count as progress in the future. Third, following on from the second point, we agree that progress is not a concept that critical theory can simply dispense with and that we would therefore do well to develop what Forst calls a "dereified, nonteleological, nondominating, emancipatory conception of progress" (18). Fourth, I think we also agree that progress is, as Forst puts it, "not a normative concept in its own right" (20). Rather, it is normatively dependent, in the sense that it is judged relative to some kind of normative standard that can't itself be the concept of progress—or else the claim that something is an instance of progress can never be more than a self-congratulatory begging of the question.

In other words, both Forst and I are critical of what I characterize as the left-Hegelian approach to the question of normativity, an approach that seeks to ground its forward-looking understanding of progress as a moral-political imperative in a backward-looking story about progress as a "fact." But we arrive at this shared critique of the left-Hegelian-historicist approach from opposite directions, and we draw equally opposed conclusions from it. For Forst, the solution to the problem of progress is to be found in his basic normative conception of the right to justification. For him, progress can only be justified

147

if those who are subjected to the changes in the social order determine the changes through a process of justification. Thus "the justification of progress lies in the progress of justification as a social practice among equals" (22). My approach to rethinking the concept of progress, by contrast, turns on an attempt to pull apart the backward-looking and the forward-looking conceptions of it while at the same time refraining from appealing to the kind of strongly context-transcending foundationalist conception of normativity that such historicist approaches were originally designed to avoid.[2] In other words, I seek to build on the insights of the Hegelian historicizing move by rendering them more radically reflexive, while Forst rejects those insights altogether in favor of a return to a neo-Kantian deontological account of normativity.

This leads me to what I take to be the core of our disagreement, which, as it turns out, has little if anything to do with progress. As I said, Forst and I agree that critical theory should hold on to progress as a moral-political imperative, and we agree that this understanding of progress cannot be grounded in a reading of history as progress, for a combination of conceptual and political reasons. But Forst is extremely skeptical that the contextualism that I defend constitutes a viable alternative to this Hegelian strategy, and he sees no reason to give up or rethink his foundationalist alternative. There are a number of intertwined issues here, having to do with distinctions between contextualism and relativism, on the one hand, and foundationalism and universalism, on the other hand; the relationship between foundationalism and (epistemological) authoritarianism; and the limits of immanent critique and the related notion of transcendence from within.

As I understand it, contextualism is a metanormative or second-order view that concerns the justification of our first-order normative principles or commitments. The metanormative contextualist holds that such principles are grounded not in a transcendent perspective (such as a notion of practical reason as such) but rather contextually and historically. On this view, we can understand ourselves, at a first-order substantive normative level, to be committed to values such as freedom, equality, and solidarity with the suffering of others but understand these commitments at the metanormative level as rooted in a specific historical context or normative horizon rather than via an appeal to their putatively context-transcendent character. Contextualism is a metanormative position that is perfectly compatible with the endorsement of first-order normative principles such as a principle of reciprocal equality, just as epistemological contextualism is compatible with the holding of certain claims to be true. The opposite of contextualism is therefore not universalism—for, in my view, normative commitments that we take to be universal in the scope of their application can be contextually grounded or justified—but rather foundationalism. This is another way of saying that metanormative contextualism need not go hand in hand with moral relativism or particularism. In the absence of some sort of argument for why this distinction cannot be maintained, then, it seems to me that it is misleading for Forst to characterize my position as relativist or particularist and to frame the debate between us as a choice between contextualism and universalism.

Indeed, I think that Forst and I share the aim of developing a truly self-reflexive and critical universalism; our disagreement concerns what is required for or entailed by this conception of universalism. Forst seems to think that it is sufficient to restate the basic Kantian conception of practical reason in a way that shows this conception to cohere with the logic of social struggles for emancipation. I think that a truly radically reflexive and self-critical universalism is one that understands the dangers of underwriting universalism with an abstract, formal foundationalism that claims once and for all to prescind from all particular, cultural commitments and entanglements in relations of power. A truly self-critical and reflexive universalism would acknowledge the force of what I call the pessimistic induction argument against the Kantian conception of practical reason.[3] To be clear, the point of this argument is *not* to claim that because the notion of practical reason has been defined in exclusionary and dominating ways in the past that it is *necessarily* or *nothing more than* a tool of domination. Rather, the point is the more modest one that the realization that all our previous conceptions of practical reason have been exclusionary and dominating should undermine our confidence that our own conception of practical reason actually succeeds in transcending such entanglements. In other words, it should undermine our faith in the very idea of practical reason as such and instead compel us to understand our commitment to universalism in contingent and contextual rather than transcendent or foundational terms.[4]

150 Forst sees serious problems in my defense of contextualism, however. Perhaps most concerning is his claim that my view implies that "modernity is the true normative source of universal freedom, equality, and respect and that other cultures are not really participating in this history, or if they are, they do so primarily as victims of the oppressive implications of these values historically understood" (23). If this is correct, metanormative contextualism ends up stuck in the very same Eurocentric move that I critique in theories of progress. If this were the case, it would indeed constitute a serious problem for my position. However, nowhere do I claim that modernity is the true or exclusive normative source of these values, nor do I suggest that it is a fixed or closed horizon to which no one else has access. With respect to the former point, my claim is simply that freedom, equality, and respect are values that are central to modernity's self-understanding—which is not to say that they are *unique* to this legacy, nor is it to deny that they have gone tragically and woefully unrealized—and that actually living up to those values requires critical theorists to rethink certain of our normative and methodological commitments. With respect to the latter point, I acknowledge repeatedly that normative horizons, as I understand them, are open, porous, and entangled with one another.[5] Drawing on Luc Boltanski and Laurent Thévenot's work on justification, I also distinguish between internal critique—which relies on normative standards internal to a specific order of justification—and external critique—which draws on the normative standards of one order of justification to critique another.[6] Although I defend immanent critique (which I will discuss later), I do not think that this in any way requires that critique be merely internal, which is what Forst in effect suggests. As I put it in the book, external critique "neither requires nor entails reference to an overarching context of justification that transcends and unifies all of the diverse orders of justification";[7] thus critique can be external while remaining immanent. In light of this distinction, I think it is a serious distortion to suggest that I hold that "freedom and modernity [are] Western, modern values that we can use but they cannot" (26).

Forst does not only attack my contextualism; he also defends his normative foundationalism against the charge that it is epistemologically authoritarian. Far from being authoritarian, Forst insists, foundationalism alone can give us the tools that we need to resist authoritarianism. "If you want to resist oppression," he writes, "your stance better be as strong as it can be. And if you resist fascism, you do not 'invite' the fascist to see things your way in a nonfoundationalist exchange; rather, you are convinced that he is wrong and that is how you act and why you act. . . . We do not have the liberty in this world to be the contextualists Allen wants us to be" (26). Although I admire and appreciate Forst's passion, and of course I share his desire to combat fascism and oppression effectively, nevertheless I think that this criticism confuses several issues. First, keeping in mind the distinction between contextualism and relativism, there is nothing about my view that prevents a contextualist from taking a strong stand and arguing for her beliefs in the face of fascism or anything else. To repeat, contextualism concerns the ways in which our first-order normative commitments are justified at a metanormative level, not the way that they are deployed in first-order normative discourse. Second, however, this does not mean that my account of open-ended dialogue in which others are invited to take our point of view is offered as a prescription for *politics* in the face of fascism. Perhaps I am a less systematic thinker than I should aspire to be, but I don't see any position about the latter as following directly from my metaphilosophical argument. Finally, if I were to speculate about the implications of this discussion for politics, I would have to say that it strikes me as naïve to think that strong, foundationalist justifications will help us very much in the political fight against fascism and oppression. Perhaps they might be helpful for reassuring *ourselves,* but I don't think that they are likely to do very much to convince the *fascists.*

In line with his defense of foundationalism, Forst also questions what has become something of a dogma in contemporary critical theory: namely, that critique must necessarily be immanent. While recognizing that immanent critique may be valuable in certain situations, Forst insists that critique cannot be merely immanent and "the fact that a critique is immanent is neither a reason for nor a hallmark of its legitimacy" (29). Sometimes critique may need to be more radical than Forst seems to think a wholly immanent conception of critique can be, in that it may aim to call into question an entire historically developed understanding. For this it may need to be transcending or perhaps a combination of immanent and transcending. In defense of his position, Forst cites one of Adorno's worries about immanent critique—namely, that the immanent context on which such a model of critique draws is, ex hypothesi, shaped by delusion. However, he stops short of citing the dialectical flipside of Adorno's critique of immanent critique, which is his claim that "transcendent critique sympathizes with authority in its very form, even before expressing any content; there is a moment of content to the form itself. . . . Anyone who judges something that has been articulated and elaborated—art or philosophy—by presuppositions that do not hold within it is behaving in a reactionary manner, even when he swears by progressive slogans."[8] To be sure, Forst's is not a straightforward model of transcendent critique, and I think we would both agree that what is distinctive of the critical theory tradition is precisely its attempt to spell out some conception of transcendence from within—or what I would call (perhaps tendentiously) immanent transcendence. However, it remains unclear, to me at least, what exactly transcendence from within could mean for Forst. To the extent that he denies the historicity of the criteria of normativity or rational justification, as he does, for example, when he says that the demand for justification *gives rise to* rather than *emerges out of* a historical dynamic (30), it seems to me that he relies implicitly on some conception of transcendent critique, his claims to the contrary notwithstanding. But to the extent that he not only rejects a transcendent conception of pure practical reason but also denies that we can have access to the very point of view from which we could decide whether our conception of practical reason is historically necessary or historically contingent, I think he actually agrees with me (and with Adorno, by the way) that at the metanormative level, we have no choice but to be contextualists, inasmuch as he grants that we simply don't have access to the point of view from which a genuinely context-transcendent point of view could be articulated.

Throughout his essay, Forst claims that my contextualist account, despite being motivated by the thought that an openness to difference is an appropriate antidote to the problematically imperialist implications of both Hegelian reconstructivism and Kantian constructivism, ends up embracing an overly simplistic understanding of difference that paints subaltern subjects as inherently unreasonable and therefore inferior. He worries that my view thus ontologizes cultural differences and collapses into a problematic form of reverse orientalism. Forst agrees with the idea that Euro-American critical theorists should engage in dialogue with, for example, African thinkers, but he insists that what we stand to learn from this dialogue is not primarily a lesson about cultural difference but rather one about the common normative framework that we share and how this framework can be used to critique multiple and intersecting forms of transnational domination.

As a model of such an engagement, Forst closes his essay with a discussion of the work of Achille Mbembe, suggesting, at least implicitly, that Mbembe shares Forst's rationalist, neo-Kantian foundationalism and his related conception of power as noumenal. Here, however, I'm afraid I must disagree. To be sure, Mbembe criticizes simplistic attempts to revalue racial differences—on the grounds that such attempts mirror and invert the logics of racial division and hierarchies that fuel colonial racism—and he invokes universalism, justice, and common humanity as normative values that we should strive to achieve.[9] However, Mbembe makes it abundantly clear that his universalist vision does not in any way involve a straightforward rejection or disavowal of difference, precisely because to do so would be to deny the vicissitudes of our racialized history. As he puts it, "The attempt to destroy difference and the dream of imposing a single language on all are both doomed to failure."[10] This is part of the lesson that Mbembe thinks that we can still learn from Aimé Césaire and Frantz Fanon, despite his criticisms of their work.[11] Césaire's work has enduring value, for Mbembe, precisely insofar as it shows that a concern for difference—that is, a concern for the specificity of the "Black Man" and his experience—need not "lead to a *secession* from the world but rather to the affirmation of its *plurality* and the necessity of making it thrive."[12] To affirm plurality is "to rehabilitate singularity and difference" while simultaneously rejecting "abstract visions of the universal" and acknowledging that "the universal is always defined through the register of singularity,"[13] all of which leads him to conclude that "there is no absolute universal. The only universal is the community of singularities and differences, a sharing that is at once the creation of something common and a form of separation. Here, the concern for the Black Man makes sense only because it opens the way for a reimagining of the universal community."[14]

Precisely because of the deeply ingrained histories and ongoing legacies of colonial and imperial racism, Mbembe maintains that a "dual approach" is needed if we are to "articulate a new politics and ethics founded on a call for justice."[15] This dual approach entails a complicated, dialectical understanding of difference: "What we must imagine is a politics of humanity that is fundamentally a politics of the similar, but in a context in which what we all share from the beginning is difference. It is our differences that, paradoxically, we must share."[16] In light of his complex account of difference as the very ground for the formation of the in-common, it seems to me that Mbembe cannot be yoked into a defense of an abstract, formal, foundationalist conception of practical reason. There is, as he says quite clearly, no *absolute* universal. I take this to mean that there is only a *contingent* universal, one that must be continually reimagined on the basis of a sober confrontation with the deeply ingrained, historically sedimented, and racialized differences that have been imposed and reinforced through the structures and afterlives of colonialism.

To close and to come back briefly to the theme of progress, then, it seems to me that the vision of humanity that Mbembe invokes here is interestingly quite close to that put forward by Adorno in the context of his critique of progress. Adorno argues that although we have no basis for claiming that there has been progress up to now, to assume as a result that there can be no progress in the future would be to wallow in conservative despair. For Adorno, progress refers to the notion of a fulfilled humanity, and at least one reason that there has been no progress up to now is that the concept of universal humanity has thus far gone unrealized. As Adorno puts it, "No progress may be supposed that implies that humanity already existed and could therefore be assumed to continue to progress. Rather progress would be the establishment of humanity in the first place."[17] Although, to be sure, Adorno does not root his claim that humanity does not already exist in a historical analysis of colonial racism, this claim nonetheless resonates quite strongly with Mbembe's critique of colonialism's dehumanizing logics.[18] Thus Mbembe's call for the establishment of a politics of humanity, like Adorno's, can be understood as a forward-looking imperative, a plea for justice, humanity, and the project of the universal that is grounded in a sober reading of history as a story not of progress but rather of domination. However, insofar as there is no absolute universal, the project of the universal for Mbembe, unlike for Forst, cannot be presumed to be "the final destination."[19]

NOTES

1. Theodor Adorno, *History and Freedom: Lectures 1964–1965*, ed. Rolf Tiedemann, trans. Rodney Livingstone (Cambridge: Polity, 2006), 161–62.
2. For the record, I think that Forst mischaracterizes this move when he describes it as follows: "We should not be committed to any backward-looking claim to progress and yet still hold on to a contextual, forward-looking imperative of progress" (18). My claim is much more about whether our understanding of progress as a moral-political imperative can be grounded in a backward-looking claim about progress as a "fact." In other words, the concern is much more about normativity than it is about progress per se—although I do think that there are reasons to be cautious about reading history in terms of progress even if we endorse a contextualist account of normativity; for discussion, see Amy Allen, *The End of Progress: Decolonizing the Normative Foundations of Critical Theory* (New York: Columbia University Press, 2016), 225–29.
3. See Allen, *End of Progress*, 136–45.
4. See Judith Butler's contributions to Ernesto Laclau Butler and Slavoj Žižek, *Contingency, Hegemony, Universality: Contemporary Dialogues on the Left* (London: Verso, 2000).
5. Allen, *End of Progress*, 157–58, 218.
6. Ibid., 158.
7. Ibid.
8. Theodor Adorno, *Problems of Moral Philosophy*, ed. Thomas Schröder, trans. Rodney Livingstone (Stanford: Stanford University Press, 2001), 146.
9. See Achille Mbembe, *Critique of Black Reason*, trans. Laurent Dubois (Durham: Duke University Press, 2017), 78–102 and 156–83.
10. Ibid., 94.
11. As an aside, the fact that Mbembe embraces, albeit somewhat cautiously and critically, Fanon's account of the role of emancipatory counterviolence in the overthrow of colonialism speaks pretty strongly against Forst's suggestion that Mbembe shares his noumenal conception of power. See ibid., 165–70.
12. Ibid., 157.

13. Ibid., 158.
14. Ibid.
15. Ibid., 178.
16. Ibid.
17. Adorno, *History and Freedom*, 146.
18. See Mbembe, *Critique of Black Reason*, 85–87.
19. Ibid., 183.

CHAPTER 10

Navigating a World of Conflict and Power

Reply to Critics

Rainer Forst

The world is not thy friend nor the world's law.

—WILLIAM SHAKESPEARE, *ROMEO AND JULIET*

Even though I think that Shakespeare is right and that in life as well as in philosophy, we have to navigate a world that is not only barely known to us but also often hostile and inhospitable, the great honor that my friends and colleagues bestowed on me when they so graciously commented on my work in this symposium speaks otherwise. But I consider it an exceptional occasion and an outstanding privilege that they did so, and thus I'm humbled by this great gift—and by the challenge of responding. This is not only because in my work I have learned so much from these great minds but because they have confronted me with questions to which I may not have the correct responses. So I write this in a spirit of immense gratitude and awareness of finitude, in an attempt to provide the best possible answers—but the answers must be seen for the most part as constructions on new terrain, not as repetitions of things said previously. What more could one wish for in a symposium devoted to one's work? Thus I would like to thank Eduardo Mendieta and Amy Allen in particular for organizing the workshop at Penn State in April 2017, which was so enjoyable, as well as all the participants and contributors for devoting so much time and *Geist* to my work. May it one day merit such attention.

I will try to organize my responses around three clusters of issues. On a certain reading, John Christman, Mattias Iser, and Catherine Lu all address variations on the theme of alienation; in particular, they point to different aspects of my account of justification not as overcoming but, on the contrary, as producing individual and social forms of alienation. This is a serious challenge, which I address in section 1. In section 2, I try to discuss the complex questions regarding my notion of power and domination raised by John McCormick and Melissa Yates. They probe deeply into the very nature of power as well as into the range of power relations—and relations of justification. In the final section, I return to the theme of universalism, as both a political and a moral issue situated in social struggles for emancipation in a variety of contexts. My hope is that my responses to Sarah Clark Miller and Amy Allen will help us achieve greater clarity on the notion of "critical universalism" in which we all share an interest.

The chapters raise many points and are quite diverse. But in a certain sense, there is a common thread running through them all, which provides me with an opportunity to distinguish more clearly than in my previous work between a descriptive-empirical analysis of a normative order as (possibly) an order of domination and ideology and a normative argument about what form a normative order should assume in order to be justified. During my many years of work on these issues, this categorical difference between forms of discourse has led to many misunderstandings. All too often, I have been read as asserting that existing normative orders of justification are well-ordered and happy structures of justification or that we live lives of autonomy, mutual recognition, and moral respect. In fact, my view is precisely the opposite, but I want to reconstruct the basis of such criticism of given normative structures, and how that basis can be reconstructed is the real theme of the discussions contained in this volume. Without such critical, reflexive work, without the reconstruction of what justice and autonomy mean for us as the beings we can be, a critical theory would not be possible. The distinction I want to make is not between an ideal and nonideal theory but between the factual and the counterfactual. Normative theory becomes problematic when it mistakes the latter for the real, whereas realism becomes problematic when it leaves no room for the normative.

1. JUSTIFICATION AND ALIENATION

a.

It gives me particular pleasure to discuss my ideas on the relationship between autonomy and justification with John Christman because his work sets the standards for contemporary philosophical attempts to theorize personal autonomy.[1] He addresses the question of the relationship between autonomy as a relation to oneself—that is, as a practice of self-justification—and autonomy as a relation to others as part of practices of intersubjective justification. If I understand him correctly, his critique of Kantian accounts such as mine points to two problems of alienation: first, the possible lack of fit between a person's "authentic practical identity" (45) or basic personal—in my language, "ethical"—commitments, on the one hand, and the demands of what he calls "impersonal" (47) Kantian-style morality, on the other. Does the demand to heed the priority of morality alienate persons from their deepest commitments—or what Bernard Williams used to call their "ground projects"?[2] The second problem of alienation potentially inherent in my view, according to Christman, is that in a society marked by severe structural injustice, say, of racism combined with class and gender, to assume that there is a fit between an ethical, personal identity and the public demands of political justification is an idealization. In such a society, the different kinds of self-trust, as well as social trust, that are required if citizens are to accept the demands of public justification and not see them as "an alien force" (54) imposed on them that disrespects their autonomy cannot develop.

Although these two points are well-taken and are extremely important for my approach, I think that they point in different directions. I believe that only if we provide an account of the priority of morality as a possibly "alienating" force in our ethical and political

160

lives and as demanding that we respect others as equal normative authorities can we understand and criticize the alienation and lack of trust within unjust societies. Thus the first alienation charge criticizes the priority of the kind of morality that grounds the social criticism of the second. That is a conundrum that needs to be solved if we are to develop a coherent account of alienation and social criticism.

Let me explain. Like Christman, I conceive of autonomy as the capacity to be guided by reasons that one can affirm or are one's own— or in his words, reasons one can accept "without alienation" (38). And like him, I think that such self-justification is related to justification practices within social contexts because we do not form our basic commitments on our own in isolation from those of others. We are members of families, groups of friends, religious communities, social groups and projects, political communities, and the moral community of all human beings. In *Contexts*[3] as well as in later works, I argue that the question of autonomy can be analyzed in relation to each of these various contexts—ethical, legal, political, and moral—as well as in a comprehensive way that tries to unite these contexts, as the task of finding a generally justified path of action and self-guidance. And here there might be a point of difference between us. While Christman stresses the personal unique identities and autonomy of persons, their "authentic" (42) practical identities, and argues that a nonalienated form of personal and social life requires that one be guided by one's "*own* reasons" (42)—and thus regards the demands of political as well as moral justification as demands that potentially question this kind of nonalienated self-relation—I think that we need a more contextual and complex account of autonomy.

My reasons for this are as follows. If we consider ethical autonomy to mean—very much in line with Christman—that a person can reflectively endorse her commitments and the values that guide her in her life and act on their basis, we should also take legal, political, and moral autonomy into account.[4] The norms relevant in these contexts are not alien forces, since they stem from a communal membership— although in this case, membership in a legal, political, and moral community. None of the latter are mere abstractions, although they are more abstract than ethical communities (however, it makes a big difference whether the community in question is a family or a church such as the Roman Catholic Church, which is quite a big community) and they can be treated descriptively as well as in an idealized way. Being a member of a legal community, for example, comes with specific commitments, rights, duties, and expectations—as does membership of a political or moral community. In fact, I think that showing proper respect to others whom your actions affect morally in a certain situation is not an abstract or "impersonal" imperative but one of the most personal aspects of social life. So I neither think that the demand of public justification in a political community is "grounded in an impersonal viewpoint," nor that the demand of moral respect stems from an "impersonally grounded moral law" (47). Rather, they are both aspects of a person's autonomy in a (proper) democracy of political self-government and in the "kingdom of ends," materialized in everyday situations of moral action, as part of moral reflection and self-legislation. These aspects of our autonomy are as real as our ethical commitments, and all of them are part of social practices.

However, the alienation problem cannot be discussed away; rather, the prior analysis sheds a new light on it, for while Christman tends to construct personal autonomy along ethical, particular lines, thereby bringing it closer to an authentic self-relation that can view the demands of political or moral justification as alienating, I regard the problem he points to not as one between autonomy and interpersonal justification but instead as one *immanent* to the different dimensions of autonomy. I think that this is the more realistic description and not a stylized idealistic one, for then it becomes apparent that moral autonomy can indeed have an alienating—or better, *decentering*—effect, because this is what is implied by a synthetic notion of autonomy that combines ethical and moral autonomy. If, for example, we ask a devout Catholic to accept the basic right to same-sex marriage to which she objects deeply, we are doing two things. We are asking her to reflect on whether her basic ethical commitments are too narrow and parochial and stereotypical, which is how I interpret Christman's demand of reflexivity (43), and in addition to this reflection within the realm of ethical autonomy, we are asking her to reflect morally on whether she has good reasons as a member of a political as well as of the "noumenal" moral community

162

of free and equal persons to impose her ethical views on others, possibly by law. Yes, that does mean "deep and painful conflict" and "internal resistance" (43), as Christman argues, and there is a danger of alienation, but this is the alienation that moral reflection might entail for a bigot or someone who lacks moral reasons that take equal respect into account. Hence some alienation is bad, as, for example, when people lose their self-confidence and self-trust as, say, victims of social injustice (a point to which I will return), but some alienation is unavoidable if we take seriously the demand of moral autonomy—namely, to be able to act on the basis of reciprocally and generally nonrejectable reasons because of the concrete respect we owe to others as equals.

Unlike some Kantians, I do not argue that overcoming narrow-minded ethical reasons in favor of moral ones is experienced as a true liberation by persons, for I believe that there is a serious conflict here. I also believe that personal happiness sometimes speaks in favor of not following moral reasons, and thus I take a rather tragic view of such conflicts. But I still regard them as internal to autonomy and not as conflicts between autonomy and providing justifications to others, and I also see the value in morally questioning ethical commitments, even if they are deep. This is what moral reflection does, and in many instances, it has a decentering and "alienating" force, but such alienation can give rise to learning processes, such as overcoming bigotry. To express this differently, neither Christman nor I would want to grant a fascist a valid claim to have his self-justification, ethical commitments, and nonalienated practical identity preserved and respected so that his self-trust will not be damaged by imperatives of mutual justification. If we speak as critical theorists, such identities need to be questioned and decentered, and some process of alienation might be unavoidable as a result. Anyone who has tried to convince her parents about her choice of a life path with which the parents disagree knows what this involves, and in social conflicts, this is a constant struggle. Sometimes alienation is a requirement of autonomy rather than its enemy, and that includes the self-alienation that is familiar from processes of overcoming one's own blindness.

That is why I perhaps should not agree in general with Christman when he says that "social and political practices of public justification must operate in a way that allows participants to accept them from the point of view of their own practical identities" and must not drive a "wedge" between the demands of justice and respect for autonomy (52–53). Sometimes we must drive such a wedge, because otherwise racism, sexism, and dominant classes produce and reproduce the very kind of social structures that lead to the second sort of alienation that Christman rightly mentions—namely, the alienation of persons who are victims of structural injustice and thus cannot trust the dominant structures and processes of justification, on account of their potentially ideological and dominating character. I am in complete agreement with him that we need a realistic and sober description of such social structures, but I also stress that realism requires that we distinguish the kind of alienation that a fascist experiences when he finds himself confronted with demands for democratic justification from the alienation a victim of racism suffers when asked to accept the rules of the so-called democratic game that merely reproduces the domination to which he or she is subjected. And in order to make that distinction, the normative structure of justification and the demand for justificatory respect among normative equals must be in place.

In a recent paper on alienation, I distinguished between two forms of being disrespected and disrespecting oneself as an equal normative authority, or what I call "noumenal alienation": first-order noumenal alienation means not being respected as a moral and/or political equal, and second-order alienation means not respecting oneself as such an equal.[5] As I show with reference to Rousseau, Kant, and Marx, the second form is not a necessary result of the first. And as I also argue, this analysis does not require any notion of authenticity or the good life; all that one needs is a deontological notion of being on an equal standing with others. I agree with Christman that when this requirement is violated, the result can be a lack of social and political trust, as well as of self-trust, and the social structure, as a whole or in part, appears as an "alien force" (54). But to avoid or overcome this, the imperative that there must be an "overlap between persons' ethical commitments and the values inherent in the social practices of justification" (55) may be less useful than the imperative of strict equal respect for every person as a normative authority, as the Kantian point of view requires. Otherwise, we lack the critical basis required to identify injustice and to demand respect from everyone. Sometimes, overcoming the alienation caused by injustice means alienating those who perpetuate injustice.

164

b.

Mattias Iser's contribution follows up nicely on the theme of the alleged alienating implications of my account of justification, this time with reference to my conception of toleration. In the many years in which I had the pleasure to work with him in Frankfurt, I always admired how Iser tries to combine Kantian and Hegelian insights into a unified theory of social struggle and progress.[6] In his contribution to this volume, this characteristic reappears in the form of a challenge: he is concerned that even my "respect conception" of toleration implies a problematic and normatively deficient—let us say, an alienated—form of respect that lacks, if not a necessary, then at least a highly desirable esteem component. I welcome this criticism because it requires me to confront an issue that I have not dealt with sufficiently clearly in the past.

Iser focuses on the "objection component" of the respect conception.[7] This states that those who tolerate the beliefs or practices of others out of respect among equals still find these beliefs and practices objectionable and, in an important sense, false or wrong. Particular religions view each other as false, for example, or regard atheism or blasphemy as seriously wrong or regard the life of, let us say, an investment banker who is mainly interested in reaping economic benefits as impoverished. Iser is concerned that even in a society in which "everyone is accorded equal rights and liberties as well as equal opportunities" (60), a majority could despise a minority, as in his fictional example of *Enlightened Despisistan,* which would cause unacceptable harm. So he asks which objections are admissible in a just society of equal respect and also what expressions objections can take. Where is the boundary between the racist objections that I criticize as incompatible with respect toleration and other negative views, and which expressions of objection are harmful? Furthermore, doesn't justice demand some kind of esteem of other people's valuable contributions to society? In sum, Iser argues for an "imperfect duty of esteem learning" (60) that brings the respect conception closer to the esteem conception of toleration.

These are important issues that require me to clarify what the respect conception does and does not do. In the first place, it is true that I argue for the respect conception based on a notion of what justice toward minorities demands, but that notion does not amount to a comprehensive ideal of the just society. As in every conception of toleration, such a society involves deep ethical and social conflict, which makes the term *pluralism* sound like a euphemism. Groups regard each other with reservations, criticism, and strong disapproval. That is why Goethe's saying "To tolerate means to insult"[8] mainly characterizes the hierarchical permission conception of toleration; however, by comparison with an ideal of republican unity that transcends cultural boundaries, for example, Goethe's saying also holds for respect toleration, since the latter does involve objection and disapproval. This is one of the major themes of my debate, for example, with Wendy Brown.[9] Still, according to the respect conception, the "insults" are constrained by legal, political, and cultural norms of mutual respect, which brings me to a necessary clarification. A tolerant society of respect not only accords basic rights and social justice; it also has an ethos of respect that is also an ethos of toleration. Thus such a society has to strike a balance between conflict or mutual criticism, on the one hand, and democratic community or recognition, on the other. This is Iser's concern. He thinks that I try to accommodate too much conflict and mutual contempt within the limits of justice, but I fear that his ideal of a just society is excessively communitarian.

First, Iser says that equal rights as well as equal opportunities are granted in *Enlightened Despisistan*. So does this mean that in a just society, persons can condemn the beliefs and ways of life of others? In my view, it does. People can call other religions false and the lifestyle of an investment banker impoverished and selfish (assuming that such a profession would still exist in a just society, which may be doubted). Could this reach a point where such expressions of contempt become harmful? Indeed it could. However, it is difficult to determine when this point is reached. In order to identify it, we need to distinguish between different forms of harm. Investment bankers or selfish CEOs could feel harmed because a majority of people look down on them. Still, this

166

would not involve any injustice, only a social dynamic that potentially leads to psychological pain and suffering. But consider, by contrast, a vulnerable religious minority that is despised by a majority. In this case, the harm might be substantive, since it could involve not just suffering but also social exclusion and discrimination. The respect conception must say something about such a case, and Iser is right to press me on this. But what it must say is that such forms of social exclusion are wrong because they violate mutual respect and the requirements of justice, such as the demand for equal opportunities. If the objections against certain ethnic groups, for example, go so far that members of these groups cannot find jobs or are socially stigmatized, resulting in exclusion from essential social institutions and possibilities, respect and justice are violated. But contrary to Iser, this does not mean that an imperative of esteem arises here. No such demand exists as a demand of justice. The exception is what Iser calls "accomplishment esteem" (67), which is required for social justice and equal opportunities, because positions must be open to persons based on their qualifications, and the latter must be assessed or esteemed without exclusivist prejudice. But this kind of esteem—for example, for certain skills—is not a form of cultural esteem, such as a particular regard for a certain religion. Nondiscrimination does not call for such cultural esteem.

So I agree that the ethos of respect has implications for social recognition, but it does not imply a duty to esteem others and to refrain from regarding their views as wrong and their practices as misguided. Still, Iser correctly points out that I qualify the objection component (which, to recall, is part of the respect conception). I do so because the appropriate response to racists is not to require them to be "tolerant" of persons with other ethnic backgrounds but to demand that they abandon their racism because racism violates basic forms of respect and thus cannot be reconciled with the respect conception. The same is true of homophobia. Remember that the respect conception is founded on respect for others as normative equals in spite of ethical objections to their beliefs, and the racist refuses to accord that kind of respect.

I am therefore not sure that I understand Iser's description of a tolerant racist who thinks some "races" are inferior but nevertheless respects all members of these groups as equals based on "our common humanity" (67). The respect conception, to recall, requires persons to respect each other within the bounds of justice for the right reasons, not grudgingly or for strategic reasons.

167

I also do not deny that some expressions of ethical objections can undermine "the social status and/or the self-conception" (70) of others. This is another point where I need to be clearer than in the past. Objections that undermine the social status of persons in ways that infringe on their equal citizenship rights and possibilities are impermissible, though it is very difficult to determine at what point expressions of ethical objections overstep the boundary to injustice. Today, many right-wing extremists complain that liberal or left-wing criticism and exclusion has such a character, and we need to take a closer look at such empty charges and their ideological functions. Moreover, as I indicated, I do not deny that the self-conception of persons can suffer from criticism, and this can be true of a good painter or a bad one, of a shameless CEO or a devout Muslim. In a society of respect, people have an imperfect duty not to inflict unjustified pain, but in a pluralistic and conflictual society that allows for free speech and mutual criticism, some of these consequences will be unavoidable. The pain of those who feel profoundly insulted by caricatures that ridicule the founder of the religion in which they believe is understandable, and even though a society of respect should aim to minimize such pain, it is sometimes a fact of life if basic liberties are to be guaranteed.

So I agree that we have not only a strict duty of justice to respect others as normative equals despite ethical differences but also an imperfect duty to be part of and to practice an ethos of respect that avoids insults and harm, though in an open society (if I may use that term), exercising free speech and voicing dissent and criticism are also values. Social tranquility should not be accorded priority over social criticism. This ethos includes avoiding and overcoming racial, sexist, and other demeaning stereotypes but as a matter of respect, not of esteem. It is admirable if one sees value in other religions or forms of life, as Iser argues, following Taylor (71), but I would not want to ask the atheist who may have just left an oppressive religion to seek such value in all religions. As Iser argues, one has a duty to listen to others and to try to understand their arguments in political and legal discussions and not to answer on the basis of stereotypes, but that is less than a duty to esteem these others. Sometimes we have to accept that the ethical differences between us are unbridgeable—yet morality must always be a bridge to the other. The former kind of alienation is a fact of life in pluralistic societies, the result of a long history of struggles and conflicts that did not disappear, as those who hoped to overcome religious difference and form a religion of reason had hoped.[10]

c.

Catherine Lu sheds light on a third danger of alienation resulting from (or at least overlooked by) too rigid a version of justificatory autonomy—namely, what she calls "existential alienation" (78). In her work, she masterfully shows the complex dimensions of a nonreductive politics of justice in the national and the international realms, pointing out the often invisible dangers of perpetuating structures of colonization in spite of attempts to overcome them.[11] She is concerned about the danger of reifying the idea of a structure of justification as the correct expression of political and moral autonomy in such a way that it could turn against the very collective autonomy it highlights: if we follow a certain model of a justificatory normative order, especially one that emphasizes basic rights, it could be argued that justice demands "international or external actors overriding the collective self-determination to some already marginalized or disadvantaged groups whose social practices may come into conflict with such standards" (77). But Lu's worry is not just one about a loss of political autonomy; rather, she stresses the "good of nonalienation" (79) of such groups, which she considers to be less a demand for justice than an "ethical claim" (90)—that is, a claim based on the existential and ethical preconditions for a meaningful life and for autonomy. Both worries—the loss of autonomy and the loss of meaning—present powerful challenges to my view, and I am grateful to have an opportunity to reflect on them.[12]

168

I will begin with the first question about the relation between a model of political autonomy and the practice of political autonomy—or rather, the charge of inadvertent neocolonialism. This touches on the questions of progress I discuss in the opening chapter of this volume.[13] The theory of moral and political justification that I put forward is based on the autonomy of humans as constructive agents of justification, which in a political context means that the members of a particular community are the subjects of justification of its basic structure—although not in isolation from others, since the decisions of political communities can have many consequences for nonmembers. Autonomy as justification is thus a practice; autonomy is a matter not of having a good justification served up to you by others but of being part of the construction of these justifications as a normative equal. Likewise, developing a structure of justification is a collective task of persons who, to put it in apparently paradoxical terms, autonomously construct the legal and political conditions of the exercise of their autonomy. The paradox here is only apparent because every development of—and improvement on—a basic structure of justification must proceed by collective action while at the same time shaping future collective action. Justification is a practice, not a result or a state of affairs. So there are no abstract models of what constitutes a structure of justification that could be imposed upon collectives, and there is no international authority that can infer a right to intervene when a political community fails to establish a structure of justification. Criticism of such failures, whether by internal or external agents, is appropriate, but the leap to certain "forms of intervention" (82) is impermissible because intervention is all too often a form of domination, even if it is justified as promoting democracy.[14] Here I agree with Lu at the normative level, even though I worry that some critics of "external" critique—not Catherine Lu, to be sure—have internalized the very Bush doctrine of (allegedly) "legitimate" intervention that they aim to criticize. There is no justificatory relation between external critique and external intervention—and engaging in the former in no way commits one to the latter. That is the mistake of that false doctrine, not, for example, a mistake of a normative account of human rights. That being said, to fail to recognize that certain interventions can be justified in response to grave violations of human rights or extreme aggression would be to argue in a historical void. Is there any need to mention the war on the Nazi regime in this context?

170   So I do not see any danger of justifying "usurpation or coercive interference in political communities if the external (national or international) regime asserts an objectively more justified standard of justice than the internal model" (83), as Lu fears. That would be to overlook the argument about justificatory autonomy and turn it into a consequentialist, reified model of a just social structure that is "objectively" valid and obliges communities to follow it. The right to justification as a right to a practice of justification that is autonomously developed and exercised speaks against that. So in response to Lu's question concerning how important it is that agents *themselves* practically define their basic structure, my answer is that it is essential. Only extreme forms of the denial of rights to justification raise the question of legitimate interference—which again needs to be justified within appropriate structures of justification, not by turning a deontological autonomy argument into a consequentialist argument for intervention to "produce" justice.

It is true, however, that the normative ground of a right to justification places constraints on what counts as "autonomous" self-government. Again, even if we free our minds of the specter of intervention, as we should, we still need to reflect on what these constraints are. The claim of a community to be self-governing cannot be compatible with a restrictive notion of "self" that excludes women, some ethnic groups, and the young, for example, and even if there were a high degree of acceptance of such exclusions among the excluded, one should query the situation of justification under which this acceptance is produced. Collective self-determination must mean something if it is to have justificatory value; otherwise, a traditionalist regime could also claim the right to pursue an oppressive path of development of its own.

At this point, Lu introduces the idea of "existential nonalienation." In her view, this is not another component of moral and political autonomy; rather, it is a certain way of relating to one's self as part of a particular group and of experiencing the existence of a certain meaningful collective way of life as essential for one's own life. The "self" here seems to be individual and collective at the same time. Existential nonalienation is then seen as a "prerequisite" (78) for moral or political autonomy and as aiming first and foremost at the "good of nonalienated human flourishing" (79), in line with Rahel Jaeggi's account of alienation as a disruption of possibilities of relating meaningfully to the world.[15] I see the point of this when it comes to explaining the importance of communal forms of life for indigenous groups who are trying to establish noncolonial forms of life, but I am not sure how to accommodate this good of nonalienation in a normative argument for justificatory autonomy. If it really is a *precondition* of autonomy, the same danger that Lu just pointed out with respect to my view arises: Who delivers this good if it is a precondition of autonomy? Can it be delivered paternalistically from the outside while ignoring autonomy, if there are "objectively" better accounts of a nonalienated collective life in line with certain traditions or other standards of flourishing? If, as Lu argues, "the transformation of social structures toward justice must surely require establishing conditions of possibility for agents to overcome existential alienation" (88) and if that is the precondition for moral and political autonomy, then this "transformation" and "establishing" cannot be achieved in an autonomous way, and this gives rise to the very problem of heteronomous determination by others that Lu criticized with respect to my view.

Second, I do not deny that leading a nonalienated life is an important good, though there are many forms that such a life can assume, and I also think that the good life often thrives on heteronomy as well as alienation, but I leave that aside. Still, I wonder what kind of normative weight the argument can carry. If—to connect this to my debate with Christman earlier—there are extremely patriarchal, exclusivist, caste-hierarchy-based, or other asymmetrical forms of life that claim the right to be continued as a matter of existential nonalienation, what follows from that? Again, I wonder how that kind of nonalienation could ever be a precondition for overcoming noumenal alienation, as Lu argues, if it did not have the structural features that define noumenal nonalienation—that is, to be respected (by yourself and others) as a justificatory authority equal to others.

Thus in my view, it is not a general precondition of autonomy but a component of it. I don't think Lu would disagree, since she considers existential nonalienation to be relevant only as a prerequisite for "becoming autonomous agents" (79). Thus I take it that patriarchal, racist, and nondemocratic forms of "meaningful" collective life are being ruled out—or if they are not, that Lu would have to say that the good of existential nonalienation is a good that rivals the good of autonomy. She does not argue for the latter view, and hence I think that the good of nonalienation must be seen as a component of noumenal nonalienation, not as a separate ethical good and not as a good that takes priority.

Again, as I argued earlier in response to John Christman's concerns, the issue of alienation is not to be taken lightly. As Lu, Lear, and others argue, indigenous peoples have suffered from a loss of their social worlds in many respects, also as a loss of ethical orientation and existential meaning. Such losses are tragic not only on account of the violence with which these changes were brought about and of the humiliation and exploitation involved but also because often there is no way to reconstruct these lifeworlds or to compensate for their loss. Lu discusses such questions and tragedies in her work in much greater detail and with much greater knowledge and imagination than I could muster here, but I am inclined to locate the wrong of colonialism primarily in the injustice of denying any justificatory standing to the groups and ways of life that were seen as worthless or as objects of foreign rule and domination.[16] The loss of meaning and existential orientation goes along with this and exacerbates the wrong. But it is not a separate wrong from processes of domination because the struggles of women or other groups for emancipation are often unjustifiably rejected on the grounds that they "destroy" traditional contexts of meaning and orientation, and we need criteria to distinguish such processes with respect to their emancipatory qualities. I see no other criteria apart from those of justificatory autonomy. Ethical nonalienation can be a precondition for autonomy, but it can also be a precondition for the denial or loss of autonomy, depending on the life-form one is part of. In contexts of domination, it is a good we need to treat with care, since, to use Lu's words in an opposite direction, it can continue to be a source "of intersubjective domination" (90).

2. CONTEXTS OF POWER

a.

In his work generally but especially in his readings of Niccolò Machiavelli, John McCormick is a genuine authority when it comes to analyzing the dynamics of political and social power.[17] Thus it is especially gratifying that he has commented on my notion of "noumenal power," which has received quite a bit of attention recently.[18] McCormick reconstructs my ideas here very well but fears that I overstate the role of reason giving when it comes to understanding political power in particular and that I focus too narrowly on the intentionality of the exercise of power. I understand the thrust of these points and will do my best to explain (and expand) my view.

The main idea of noumenal power is quite simple. I think that to exercise power is to make other subjects think and/or act in a certain way intended by the power-holder. Simply put, when you exercise power, you lead others to believe or do something you want them to believe or do, and you do this by certain means that make them think or act in the way you want. So they are still agents, regardless of whether the means you used were a (credible) threat, a lie, a good recommendation, or a certain look. So power works on at least minimally free agents who could still refuse your threat, though possibly at a high cost to them, and exercising power is the attempt to determine the space of reasons for others—sometimes for their benefit but sometimes in order to dominate them. If you dominate others, you limit or try to close their space of reasoning and to colonize it with certain beliefs (e.g., ideological ones); if you are a revolutionary who wants to open the eyes of these people, you try to decolonize that space of justifications. So power works on and within that space, but it does not necessarily work—as I have occasionally been mistakenly assumed to argue (though not by McCormick)—through reflexive reasons or good justifications. Power *produces* a justification for those who are its subjects, but it often does so by means of manipulation—that is, by hidden mechanisms that produce justifications in others but not in a justified and openly discursive way. Power operates on people's beliefs and their space of reasons but *not* necessarily through rational reason giving. It works if others "accept" the justifications you "gave" them, and that includes modes of communicative reason giving as well as ideological delusion. The general concept of noumenal power is meant to serve as a basis for distinguishing such modes of the exercise of power.

So McCormick is right to say that the power-holder "provides" the subject of power with reasons (96), since a threat only works as an exercise of power if it is credible, and credibility is a noumenal term; *credere* means "to believe." And he is right when he interprets me as saying that the means through which power is exercised are very diverse. But he is concerned about how specific our conception of the intention of the agent who exercises power must be. I try to distinguish the *exercise* of *power* as an intentional form of influencing or motivating others from unintended effects that I call mere *influence*—so I occasionally use the word *influence* in both contexts, as McCormick remarks (98), but I trust that the difference is clear enough. If people act because they think that I wanted them to act in a particular way but I in fact did not, one should not call that an exercise of power on my part but a power effect or a case of me unintentionally influencing others.

Does it suffice to change other people's mental state but not their behavior? That depends on what you intend. If you want them to act in a certain way based on some beliefs you produced in them and they don't, then the right belief may not have been produced. But sometimes it can suffice to just change people's minds without intending that they should act in any particular way, as in the well-taken example of a teacher who wants to strengthen certain competences but intends no particular courses of action on the part of the students. That is a form of noumenal power and, if things go well, an enduring one.

It may also be that one does not intend any very specific outcome, as in McCormick's case of seduction, if one is content with just securing the positive attention of the other. But I would still say that one intends a real and not just a "*possible*" (100) change of thought and action by using the means of seduction, even if the leeway for such a change is left open from a mild to a very serious interest in you. But it is right to say, as McCormick does, that every form of power comes with a certain indeterminacy and that every intensification of power tries to limit that indeterminacy, though not only in cases of seduction that can backfire. Even with the direct threat of holding a gun to someone's head, the power game is still a game, although in this case, a very serious one, because you cannot completely determine the outcome as long as the other is minimally free to respond and refuse to act in the way you want. So I agree that teachers, lovers, or policemen use very different means of power, and as I said before, I think that the analysis of these dimensions will prove very useful, as Machiavelli taught us. The prince wants to be feared and admired. And different teachers and different policemen might also occasionally employ quite different methods of power. And so do desperate people who are trying to regain noumenal power over others in a situation of seeming powerlessness—as the Sforza example shows.

But McCormick wouldn't be a good student of Machiavelli's if he did not add a word of caution about placing too much emphasis on the use of reason giving especially in politics—even if reason giving is interpreted in that very wide way that I suggest, which includes guns as reasons. Weber's notion of power as being backed by serious threats makes a comeback in McCormick's view when he argues that in politics, those who exercise power "must treat some subjects or citizens as objects in order to guarantee the stability and even the justice of the polity" (104). We might have a discussion about the seemingly iron nature of the law of politics expressed here, but I see no reason to disagree with the basic idea that in politics, acts of violence—using others as mere objects—often (and indeed most of the time) have a noumenal intention and effect. As McCormick says, acts of public violence aim to "deter" (ibid.) people or to "satisf(y)" a population hungry for authority (ibid.). All these are noumenal effects of the display of the power to exercise violence. But if the violence is used to kill the object of the exercise of force, it becomes mere violence because the person who is killed is no longer the object of an attempt to make him or her do something the power-holder wants. So those in power exercise pure violence—and not further power—over the person to be killed; the public act of violence is therefore at once a feast of power[19] and an admission of its limits. That is one reason those who are executed can become heroes, as McCormick says. I agree with his general conclusion that in politics, the use of violence often aims to stabilize noumenal power through fear and sometimes through appeals to justice or revenge. The distinction between noumenal power and pure violence actually helps here, I think.

b.

In her genuinely thought-provoking contribution, Melissa Yates poses a particularly vexing question for someone like me who argues that we should track existing relations of rule and/or domination beyond established contexts of justice within state boundaries or other legal-political institutions in order to identify the real contexts of injustice that need to be transformed into contexts of justification. The idea, as she says, is not just to politicize such relations and their possibly hidden structures of power and domination but also to transform them into relations of justification and of justice (to be established through practices of justification). Yates now takes me to task for what she calls "*transtemporal relations of political power*" (109)[20] and asks, "Can we be ruled or dominated by members of our political community who entirely preexist us, or can we dominate those to come" (117)? That is an important question, and obviously it works in both temporal directions.

I do not doubt that past generations influence us in many ways, both material and noumenal, not only through the institutions they have bequeathed to us but also by how they opened or closed the realm of justifications in which we live—not to mention the material resources they have left (or failed to leave) us. So influence is a reality and hence so too are the lasting effects of enabling or constraining structures of rule and possibly of domination. However, I hesitate to say that as a result, past generations or particular individuals still rule over or dominate us. What they did may facilitate domination here and now to a greater or lesser extent, but it does not follow that they exercise domination over us, because domination is a relation between subjects who exist in a *shared* space of justifications. We also share, Yates might reply, a space of justifications with past or future persons or groups; however, that is different from the kind of sharing implied by a social relation of power. But as I said, power effects and forms of influence certainly exist.

177

To regard ourselves as being dominated by former agents—as the examples listed by Yates suggest, by the precommitments that bind us constitutionally—would, I think, be to blame the wrong people. Although the examples cited certainly set the course for lasting structural injustices, the latter are now *our* injustices, and *we* are responsible for changing (or not changing) them. We can blame persons of the past in part for making things difficult for us, but the responsibility for accepting unacceptable structures of injustice resides with us. In a context of domination, the causes of domination must be identified correctly, as regards both structures and agency. So, yes, power does exert transtemporal effects, but there is no exercise of power or domination across time. The exercise of power is a matter of the here and now. However, as Yates points out, the transtemporal effects of power mean that we face the task of unveiling power structures that extend far into the past and may have become invisible, firmly occupying our noumenal realm.

The same holds when it comes to the future: exercises and structures of power can influence actions and events in the future, and that influence can lead to future structures of domination; however, power and domination are not exercised directly over future agents. And this influence means that we do have duties of justification toward future persons, in spite of nonexistence issues,[21] but the duties in question are not ones of reciprocal and general justification, because the reciprocity of reasons and claims cannot be established. However, we can and ought to reflect on the structures we leave behind that predetermine the lives of future persons, and we should take the *possible* views and claims of future persons into account. But it is *we* who must make the decisions, and we cannot subordinate our decisions fully to the imagined claims of an endless succession of future persons. That would involve the danger of them overpowering us, since they might be very numerous. So we have a duty of justification, though an *imperfect* one, because we must find measures to balance current and future claims, all of which will be quite diverse. I would even entertain the idea that this could be a duty that does not exist in a strictly Kantian framework— namely, an *imperfect duty of justice*—because we have a duty not to contribute to future structures of domination. But the major role played by the imagination here places limits on this duty and renders it imperfect, allowing us some leeway to find justifications that avoid future domination. We also have a duty, as part of that imperfect duty of justice, to ensure that future persons do not suffer from a lack of essential goods to live an autonomous life appropriate for them as equal normative authorities. This is also a domain in which another classical distinction does not hold—namely, the distinction between a natural duty of justice and a relational social one, since our relation to future persons does not clearly fit into these categories.

As I said, I have gone out on a limb in presenting these thoughts as something I am willing to entertain. I will need to think more about this and also about the general question Yates raises in conclusion—namely, whether we have a duty to reflect on the limits of our justificatory imagination. I think we do, as part of the work of critical reason of finite but, at the same time, self-reflecting and learning beings. Identifying the limits of our notions of justificatory communities and relations, as well as expanding these communities in the right way, is one of the major tasks of justice as justification.

3. CRITICAL UNIVERSALISM

a.

As Sarah Clark Miller suggests in her sympathetic reconstruction of my theory of transnational (in)justice, feminist criticism of transnational sexual violence is essential when it comes to understanding the specificities, as well as the general structures, of gender injustice and oppression. I agree with this and have been using feminist criticism of exclusivist forms of democracy[22] as well as of human rights violations[23] as prime examples of situated and, at the same time, context-transcending social criticism. As Miller makes very clear, both in this piece and in her work in general,[24] the two aspects must be treated together: we need a situated and context-sensitive diagnosis of gender oppression that does not work with "false universals" (132) and essentializing gender assumptions, and we should not fall prey to the "fetishization or overvaluation of the immanent" (133), for that would be to confuse the *imperative of situated criticism* with the *imperative of contextualist standards of critique*. Confusing the two would involve a false connection or inference: we should critically examine concrete cases of gender oppression and its deeper structures in various societies as well as transnationally, and we should critically examine the standards, whether local or universal, used to unveil such oppression. Sometimes universal standards can overcome the parochial nature of local standards, but sometimes local standards can uncover false and reifying universal assumptions. And false universals must be uncovered by critical universals—which raises the issue of how we arrive at critical universal norms.

Like Miller, I think that a critical theory of structural injustice has to combine the perspective of participants who suffer from such injustice with a critique of unjustifiable claims to validity, whether they assume that the exemplar of humanity is "masculine and white" (134) or, on the essentialist assumption, that all women share the same experiences—or what Miller provocatively calls "imperialist feminism" (135). Where notions of human rights have been developed that rest on such assumptions, they must be deconstructed—but as Miller rightly argues, this does not mean that we should identify the whole concept of human rights as "Western" (134) or as being doomed to be a weapon of oppression. It can be a tool for domination (such as when property rights are reified and used to trump legitimate interests) or a tool for resisting domination. There is no reason to suspect that all "universals" are oppressive and to attribute all the saving power to "local" forms of life, for that may blind us to the structures of oppression to which they give rise. Critical thinking ought to free itself from such false dichotomies and forge connections with local struggles for "true" emancipation.

But "true" emancipation ought not to be identified on the basis of a certain "ideal" form, something to which I appeal according to Miller (136); on the contrary, there is no contradiction between a transcendental counterfactual argument that stresses the right and the duty to recipro-cal and general justification and the contextual, immanent forms that such a demand for justification—or the refusal to accept dominant justifications—assumes. A *counterfactual* normative standard such as the principle of justification does not construct a model of a justified society in the mode of an "*ideal* theory" to which local practices are then compared. My approach does not involve an ideal theory but merely relies on a principle of critique that states that no normative order ought to be immune from being questioned as regards its under-lying justifications by anyone who is subject to it. Thus pace McNay's critique (which Miller cites) that reliance on a general principle of reason "shields [the approach] from systematic criticism and conse-quently constrains critique's capacity for reflexive self-scrutiny,"[25] the opposite is the case: there could be no systematic rational criticism and reflexive self-scrutiny if we did not believe that the critical faculty of reason can overcome its own blindness (though only in piecemeal fashion). Enlightenment through critique that employs standards of reciprocal and general justification is a *contextual* practice, not one sit-uated in an ideal realm, but we need *criteria* to distinguish between better and worse justifications. The idea that "we instinctively recognise oppression when we see it"[26] won't do here because instinct is not based on rational standards. I agree with McNay and Miller that, all too often, standards of "reasonable" justification reflect unjustifiable structures of domination and tend to exclude allegedly "unreasonable" voices that ought to be heard; however, this critique itself relies on the principle of reciprocal and general justification to question its own concrete forms. This constitutes critical dialectics. So I agree with Miller that my idea of an "enlightened universal" is very different from the idea of immanent criticism favored by McNay (139). The latter involves not only the danger of relativism but also the danger of "instinctively" ignoring or misinterpreting existing forms of domination because one's instincts have been formed by parochial structures of power that may dress themselves up as universally or traditionally justified.

Miller is right to identify "adaptive preferences" (140) or, in an older language, "false consciousness" as posing a vexing problem for critical theory. The problem in question has often been discussed as a dilemma between paternalism (including the ascription of "true interests" to persons) and a lack of critique precisely where domination has successfully "produced" obedient subjects. In my view, this is a case of second-order alienation, of not seeing yourself as an equal authority of justification—a thesis that does not imply that such persons necessarily experience emotional or psychological suffering (although that is possible). I do not impute true interests to such persons but only stress their status as equals, a status that no one, themselves included, should question. But this does not mean that those who are alienated in that way "forfeit" (142) their right to justification; it only means that they don't recognize that they have such a right and thus do not make use of it. Nor does it imply that we can presume to have justificatory authority over them. It only means that we ought to engage in attempts to discursively "crack" the noumenal systems that hold them captive—in a way that does not violate their normative authority. Our critique must always express the respect we owe them as equals, even if they deny such equality.[27]

b.

I am profoundly grateful to Amy Allen for continuing our conversation about critical theory in such a kind and gracious way in her reply to my reflections on progress in this volume. I have not only learned a great deal from her groundbreaking writings on power,[28] to which my own reflections on noumenal power in particular are indebted. In good dialectical fashion, I invariably learn a lot from her critical challenges, as I endeavor to come up with appropriate responses to her searching questions and counterproposals.

Allen lists our substantive agreements on a number of points, including our dialectical reading of progress. Criticism of the "ideologically imperialist and neocolonial misuses to which the concept of historical progress has been put" (147), she writes, is motivated by the hope that this critique may contribute to "real" progress toward deconstructing and overcoming these ideologies.

In the spirit of our shared membership in the critical theory family, I would add a few more dialectical points on which we may also agree.

In my view, a critique of ideology worthy of the name does not try to replace one ideology with another (as in a Nietzschean view); rather, it aims at a *rational* criticism of ideological narratives. A critical theory cannot merely focus on criticizing false standards of rationality but must for its part also employ better standards of reasonable justification. As Allen argues, if we aim at a critique of "exclusionary and dominating" (149) ways in which reason has been defined in the past, we must also aim at a "truly self-critical and reflexive universalism" (ibid.) for which reason is the relevant epistemic faculty. This is why I agree with Allen when she says that reason is not "*necessarily* or *nothing more than* a tool of domination" (ibid.), since that would make an ideology critique impossible. In that context, I am not sure that I would share Allen's characterization of her claim that "all our previous conceptions of practical reason have been exclusionary and dominating" (ibid.) as "modest." On the contrary, I find it far too general and sweeping, because it downplays the many ways in which rational critique has been effective in attacking religious, racial, gendered, or nationalist forms of unreason—whether these are dressed up as forms of reason or, as in fascism, as explicit attacks on reason. No critique of a dialectic of enlightenment that shows how one-sided and impoverished forms of "instrumental" rationality have become inverted into the opposite of reason can abandon the claim of rational criticism, including self-criticism.

Thus our major disagreement concerns whether a critique of dominating forms of reason should "undermine our faith" (ibid.) in a conception of critical reason based on the very principle of critique—which accepts no valid claims other than ones that can be reciprocally and generally justified among the participants in a social practice—and lead us to embrace "contingent and contextual" (150) standards of critique. I have my doubts because I think that reason turns into domination precisely when it affirms contextual, particular and exclusionary, standards of interpretation and justification; thus I have no confidence in any such standards apart from rational critique. Rejecting false universals does not necessarily mean embracing the parochial; rather, it can mean aiming at better justifications that overcome parochialism. Contingent and unjustifiable limits on the justification community have, in so

182

many ways, produced the horrors and injustices that Amy Allen and I regard as the targets of critical theory. Thus a Rortyan methodology[29] of pointing to the contingency of our moral language game and limiting the justification community to those who share our language and are "like us" is not a possible methodology for critical theory.

183

At this point in our conversation, Allen suggests that we should not think in terms of an opposition between contextualism and universalism but instead make a distinction between contextualism and foundationalism. This gives rise to two questions, I believe. Can there be a form of contextualist universalism, as she believes, and in what sense is my view "foundationalist"? As to the first, it seems contradictory to argue, as Allen (and Rorty) do, that one can be a first-order universalist and a second-order contextualist. That would mean that the alleged universalism can only claim to be valid for and be understood by those who share a particular social and historical context, so there would be no universalism as long as we do not all share the same social context. Allen comes close to arguing that, in the modern world, we all live in a single context, since modernity in her conception is not a "fixed or closed horizon to which no one else has access" (150), but I leave this view aside here, because in effect it would rob the term *contextualism* of its meaning. As long as a plurality of evaluative horizons and contexts exist, no single horizon can claim to ground universalism. That would be just the kind of self-inflated move that Allen and I alike criticize— possibly a form of imperialism or at least a self-congratulatory view and, in any case, a form of false universalism. My conclusion, therefore, is that for a critical theorist who should be critical of false labels, there can be no such thing as contextualist universalism.

As for "foundationalism," I don't think that this term, as Allen uses it, covers my approach. On the contrary, I believe that it captures views like Allen's, which think that metanormative contextualism is objectively true and that we know for sure (but from what standpoint exactly?) that there simply is no context, not even a noumenal one, that can be characterized as a space of reasons shared by all human beings. Thus metanormative contextualism, apart from being self-contradictory, since it asserts a universal truth about humans as purely contextual beings while denying that such transcontextual truths exist, is as foundationalist a view as the opposing one—namely, the belief that there is only one context or form of life shared by all human beings. But the latter is not what I believe. Far from arguing from a "view from nowhere," I regard humans as contextual beings, but I believe that their capacity to reason critically enables them to transcend their horizons and to achieve what Gadamer called a "fusion of horizons." Moreover, I share the Kantian view that reconstructing the rational criteria for justifying validity claims is the work of *finite* beings who engage in an exercise of reconstruction that they perform from within their local and finite perspectives, for want of any other perspective; however, they think that they have a faculty of communication and reasoning that is governed by principles that they can use for the purposes of knowledge and critique. To regard the reconstruction of these principles as a transcendental enterprise in no way turns my approach into a form of foundationalism, since (in contrast to metanormative contextualism) it does not claim to possess a God's-eye view but only to perform a finite rational reconstruction. Thus the reconstruction can be fallible,[30] but we can recognize this fallibility only if we believe that the principles of reason are reliable and binding for us, especially when overcoming our failures—to believe otherwise would render our fallibility unintelligible. Kantians are well able to distinguish between a *transcendental* argument and an absolute *transcendent* standpoint detached from finitude and context. Unlike metanormative contextualism, I have no access to a "genuinely context-transcendent point of view" (152).

That one lacks such a standpoint does not mean that one cannot engage in true and critical reflection, and engaging in such a practice presupposes that standards of rationality, normatively speaking, must be the same for all persons who make rational claims; otherwise, we would have no reason to engage in mutual understanding and criticism. Moreover, learning processes would not be possible, only conversions without reasons. Contextualism, I fear, closes or seals off spaces of reasons that we should instead try to open up or to keep open, and I think Allen and I agree on this.

I also do not think that we need a God's-eye view in order to be convinced of our moral criticism of domination, of which fascism is a particularly atrocious form. What we need instead is the rational and, at the same time, moral conviction that there can be no good reasons for placing arbitrary restrictions on the moral-justification community and not recognizing the right to justification of some persons. And it would be to misunderstand my argument to assert, as Allen does, that we need strong moral foundations for our critical claims so that we can "convince the fascists" (151). Not for a moment would I make the truth of a moral claim depend on the factual assent of a fascist. Rational argument is about the truth, not about initiating conversions, as a Rortyan perspective would have it. Questions of truth and questions of strategy are two different things.

Finally, like Allen and Mbembe, I share the view that there is a dialectical relation between singularity and universality. This is the point of a formal conception of justification that leaves the power and authority to determine how universal respect can be combined with particular forms of life to a discursive process that is not dominated by a particular, substantive norm dressed up as a universal norm. "Reimagining the universal community," to use the phrase of Mbembe's quoted by Allen (154), must be a discursive enterprise, and a critique of forms of domination must be its foremost aim. But we need criteria for what counts as domination. They do not predetermine what counts as generally and reciprocally justifiable, but they exclude all the forms of domination that violate reciprocity and generality. That is the core of rational criticism. Human beings possess no other faculty in order to overcome all forms of contextualist blindness that are dressed up as (false) universalisms or that (falsely) deny universal claims.

NOTES

1. See especially John Christman, *The Politics of Persons* (Cambridge: Cambridge University Press, 2019).
2. I discuss Williams's view in Rainer Forst, *The Right to Justification* (New York: Columbia University Press, 2012), chaps. 1 and 3.
3. Rainer Forst, *Contexts of Justice* (Berkeley: University of California Press, 2002).
4. I developed this further in my text on political liberty (now chap. 5 of *The Right to Justification*), the English version of which was first published in a volume edited by John Christman and Joel Anderson, *Autonomy and the Challenges of Liberalism* (Cambridge: Cambridge University Press, 2005), chap. 10.

5. Rainer Forst, "Noumenal Alienation: Rousseau, Kant and Marx on the Dialectics of Self-Determination," *Kantian Review* 22, no. 4 (2017): 523–51.

6. Matthias Iser, *Indignation and Progress* (New York: Oxford University Press, forthcoming).

7. See Rainer Forst, *Toleration in Conflict* (Cambridge: Cambridge University Press, 2013).

8. Johann Wolfgang von Goethe, *Maxims and Reflections* (London: Penguin, 1998), 116 (translation amended).

9. Wendy Brown and Rainer Forst, *The Power of Tolerance: A Debate* (New York: Columbia University Press, 2014).

10. See Forst, *Toleration in Conflict,* chap. 6 on the "The Enlightenment—for and Against Toleration."

11. See Catherine Lu, *Just and Unjust Interventions in World Politics: Public and Private,* paperback with a new afterword (Basingstoke: Palgrave Macmillan, 2011); Catherine Lu, *Justice and Reconciliation in World Politics* (Cambridge: Cambridge University Press, 2017).

12. For a related critique, see Melissa Williams, "On Turning Away from Justification," in *Toleration, Liberty and the Right to Justification,* by Rainer Forst (Manchester: Manchester University Press, forthcoming).

13. See my chapter 2, "The Justification of Progress and the Progress of Justification," in this volume.

14. See Dorothea Gädeke, *Politik der Beherrschung* (Berlin: Suhrkamp, 2017).

15. Rahel Jaeggi, *Alienation* (New York: Columbia University Press, 2016).

16. Compare Lea Ypi, "What's Wrong with Colonialism," *Philosophy & Public Affairs* 41, no. 2 (2013): 158–91.

17. See especially his *Machiavellian Democracy* (New York: Cambridge University Press, 2011).

18. See Amy Allen, Mark Haugaard, and Rainer Forst, "Power and Reason, Justice and Domination: A Conversation," *Journal of Political Power* 7, no. 1 (2017): 7–33; Sameer Bajaj and Enzo Rossi, "Noumenal Power, Reasons, and Justification: A Critique of Forst," in *Constitutionalism Justified,* ed. Ester Herlin-Karnell and Matthias Klatt (Oxford: Oxford University Press, forthcoming); Lois McNay, "The Limits of Justification: Critique, Disclosure and Reflexivity," *European Journal of Political Theory* (2016): https://journals-sagepub-com.ezaccess.libraries.psu.edu /doi/pdf/10.1177/1474885116670294, reprinted in the Herlin-Karnell and Klatt volume, where I will reply to these critics. See also the special issue on noumenal power in the *Journal of Political Power* 11, nos. 1–2 (2018): 1–114, 139–50, with contributions by Clarissa Hayward, Steven Lukes, Mark Haugaard, Albena Azmanova, Pablo Gilabert, Simon Susen, and Matthias Kettner, as well as my reply "Noumenal Power Revisited," forthcoming in the *Journal of Political Power.*

19. As Foucault describes it in *Discipline and Punish* (New York: Vintage, 1979).

20. See also her *Democracy as Strangers* (forthcoming).

21. See Anja J. Karnein, *A Theory of Unborn Life* (Oxford: Oxford University Press, 2012).

22. Compare Forst, *Contexts of Justice,* chap. 3.

23. See, e.g., Forst, *Right to Justification,* chaps. 9 and 11.

24. See, e.g., Sarah Clark Miller, *The Ethics of Need: Agency, Dignity, and Obligation* (New York: Routledge, 2012).

25. McNay, "Limits of Justification," 2. I reply to McNay in detail in my "The Constitution of Justification: Replies and Comments," in *Constitutionalism Justified,* ed. Ester Herlin-Karnell and Matthias Klatt (forthcoming).

26. McNay, "Limits of Justification," 14.

27. See James Tully, *On Global Citizenship* (London: Bloomsbury, 2014).

28. Amy Allen, *The Power of Feminist Theory* (Boulder: Westview, 1999); Amy Allen, *The Politics of Our Selves: Power, Autonomy, and Gender in Contemporary Critical Theory* (New York: Columbia University Press, 2008).

29. Richard Rorty, *Contingency, Irony, and Solidarity* (Cambridge: Cambridge University Press, 1989).

30. See the remarks by Habermas on Apel's foundational strategy of transcendental justification in Jürgen Habermas, *Moral Consciousness and Communicative Action* (Cambridge, MA: MIT Press, 1990), 76–98.

CONTRIBUTORS

AMY ALLEN is Liberal Arts Professor of philosophy and women's, gender, and sexuality studies and head of the philosophy department at Penn State. Her research and teaching interests include nineteenth- and twentieth-century continental philosophy (especially Marx, Nietzsche, Freud, the Frankfurt School, and Foucault and psychoanalysis), social and political theory, and feminist theory. She is the author of *The Power of Feminist Theory: Domination, Resistance, Solidarity* (Westview Press, 1999), *The Politics of Our Selves: Power, Autonomy, and Gender in Contemporary Critical Theory* (Columbia University Press, 2008), *The End of Progress: Decolonizing the Normative Foundations of Critical Theory* (Columbia University Press, 2016), and *Critical Theory Between Klein and Lacan: A Dialogue,* coauthored with Mari Ruti (Bloomsbury Press, forthcoming 2019). She has also coedited, with Eduardo Mendieta, *From Alienation to Forms of Life: The Critical Theory of Rahel Jaeggi* (Penn State University Press, 2018) and the *Cambridge Habermas Lexicon* (Cambridge University Press, 2019).

JOHN CHRISTMAN is a professor of philosophy, political science, and women's studies and director of the Humanities Institute at Penn State. He is the author of various works in social and political philosophy, including *The Politics of Persons: Individual Autonomy and Socio-historical Selves* (Cambridge University Press, 2009), *Social and Political Philosophy: A Contemporary Introduction* (Routledge, 2002), and *The Myth of Property: Toward an Egalitarian Theory of Ownership* (Oxford University Press, 1994). He is also the editor of *The Inner Citadel: Essays on Individual Autonomy* (Oxford University Press, 1989) and coeditor with Joel Anderson of *Autonomy and the Challenges to Liberalism: New Essays* (Cambridge University Press, 2005).

RAINER FORST is a professor of political theory and philosophy at the Wolfgang Goethe University, in Frankfurt am Main, Germany.

Since 2007, he is the codirector with Klaus Günther of the Normative Orders excellence cluster at the Goethe University. He was named the "most important political philosopher of this generation" when he was awarded the Wilhelm Leibniz Prize in 2012. He is the author of *Contexts of Justice* (University of California Press, 2002), *The Right to Justification: Elements of a Constructivist Theory of Justice* (Columbia University Press, 2012), *Toleration in Conflict: Past and Present* (Cambridge University Press, 2013), *Justification and Critique: Towards a Critical Theory of Politics* (Polity, 2013, with Wendy Brown), and *Normativity and Power* (Oxford University Press, 2018) and the author of over one hundred scholarly essays.

MATTIAS ISER is an associate professor of philosophy at Binghamton University, The State University of New York. He is the author of *Empörung und Fortschritt: Grundlagen einer kritischen Theorie der Gesellschaft* (Campus, 2019), already in its third edition, and winner of the 2009 Best First Book Award of the German Political Association. A translation is forthcoming with Oxford University Press. He is also a coauthor with David Strecker of *Jürgen Habermas zu Einführung* (Junius Verlag, 2010). He is presently at work on a manuscript titled *A Theory of Legitimate Violence: A Recognitional Account*. He has also edited with Gerhard Göhler and Ina Kerner *Politische Theorie: 25 umkämpfte Begriffe zur Einführung*, second edition (Verlag fur Sozialwissenschaften, 2011).

CATHERINE LU is a professor of political science at McGill University and coordinator of the Research Group on Global Justice of the Yan P. Lin Centre for the Study of Freedom and Global Orders in the Ancient and Modern Worlds at McGill. Her research interests intersect political theory and international relations, focusing on critical and normative studies in international political theory on cosmopolitanism, global justice, human rights, intervention, colonial international order, structural injustice, and alienation. She is the author of *Justice and Reconciliation in World Politics* (Cambridge University Press, 2017), which won the 2018 Robert L. Jervis and Paul W. Schroeder Best Book Award from the International History and Politics Section of the American Political Science Association, the 2018 Yale H. Ferguson Prize from the International Studies Association— Northeast Region, and was cowinner of the 2018 Sussex International Theory Prize (UK), and *Just and Unjust Interventions in World Politics: Public and Private* (Palgrave Macmillan, 2006).

JOHN P. MCCORMICK is a professor of political science at the University of Chicago. His research and teaching interests include political thought in Renaissance Florence (specifically, Guicciardini and Machiavelli), nineteenth- and twentieth-century continental political and social theory (with a focus on Weimar Germany and Central European émigrés to the United States), the philosophy and sociology of law, the normative dimensions of European integration, and contemporary democratic theory. He is the author of *Carl Schmitt's Critique of Liberalism: Against Politics as Technology* (Cambridge University Press, 1997), *Weber, Habermas, and Transformations of the European State: Constitutional, Social, and Supranational Democracy* (Cambridge University Press, 2006), *Machiavellian Democracy* (Cambridge University Press, 2011), *Weimar Thought: A Contested Legacy* (Princeton University Press, 2013), and *Reading Machiavelli* (Princeton University Press, 2018).

EDUARDO MENDIETA is a professor of philosophy, associate director of the Rock Ethics Institute, and affiliate faculty member at the School of International Affairs and the Bioethics Program at Penn State University. He is the author of *The Adventures of Transcendental Philosophy* (Rowman and Littlefield, 2002) and *Global Fragments: Globalizations, Latinamericanisms, and Critical Theory* (SUNY Press, 2007). He is also a coeditor with Jonathan VanAntwerpen of *The Power of Religion in the Public Sphere* (Columbia University Press, 2011), with Craig Calhoun and Jonathan VanAntwerpen of *Habermas and Religion* (Polity, 2013), and with Stuart Elden of *Reading Kant's Geography* (SUNY Press, 2011). Most recently, he coedited with Amy Allen *From Alienation to Forms of Life: The Critical Theory of Rahel Jaeggi* (Penn State University Press, 2018) and the *Cambridge Habermas Lexicon* (Cambridge University Press, 2019).

SARAH CLARK MILLER is an associate professor of philosophy and affiliate faculty member in bioethics and women's, gender, and sexuality studies at Penn State University. She is an ethicist who also works in social and political thought. She is a past acting and associate director and current faculty affiliate of the Rock Ethics Institute. Her recent work includes *The Ethics of Need: Agency, Dignity, and Obligation* (Routledge, 2012) and articles on global responsibility, relational dignity, harm and moral injury, genocidal rape, and reproductive ethics in journals such as *Social Theory and Practice* and *The Journal of Social Philosophy*. She is currently writing two books—one on sexual violence and a second on relational ethics.

MELISSA YATES is an assistant professor of philosophy at Rutgers University in Camden, New Jersey. Her research focuses on whether and how political power can be justified democratically to citizens. She has presented and published articles concerning the role of moral and religious conflict for liberal democratic theories, drawing largely from the legacies of John Rawls and Jürgen Habermas. She is currently working on a book project that proposes an alternate account of the challenges and opportunities for democratic governance with and as strangers, in contrast with liberal and deliberative theories of democracy focused on the pressures of resolving disagreement.

INDEX

ability, 41, 44
  See also capacity
acceptance, 39, 52, 62, 64
action, 93, 101–3
adaptive preferences, 141, 180
Adorno, Theodor W., 30, 138, 145–46, 152,
    154–55
Africa, 32–33
African Philosophy through Ubuntu
    (Ramose), 32
agency
  authenticity and, 42
  political, 114, 116–17
  power and, 97, 103, 173
  trust and, 44–45
alienation
  adaptive preference and, 142
  autonomy and, 38, 50, 84–89, 159–63,
    168–72
  esteem and, 163, 168
  existential, 87, 168, 170–73
  identity and, 43, 44, 45
  justice and, 78
  loss of freedom as, 86
  noumenal, 86, 88
  reverse orientalism and, 24–25
  second-order, 181
  self-respect and, 85
  trust and, 13
  universalism and, 27
  See also estrangement
Allen, Amy, 17–18, 22–25, 35, 94, 181–85
Apportionment Act, 119
atonement, 45
Austro Marxism, 1
authenticity, 42, 45, 50, 87, 91 n. 34, 159, 161
authoritarianism, 26, 151
authority, 44
autonomy
  adaptive preferences and, 141
  alienation and, 38, 50, 84–89, 159–63,
    168–72
  colonialism and, 81
  decisional, 82
  discursive, 32, 33

ethical, 92 n. 38
identity and, 13
justice and, 76
moral, 77–79, 89–90, 92 n. 36
  See also self-determination

Bayle, Pierre, 31
behavior, 102
Benhabib, Seyla, 30
Benjamin, Walter, 145
Black Man, the, 153–54
Boltonski, Luc, 150
Bratman, Michael, 56 n. 15
Brown, Wendy, 165

Canada, 83, 88
Canadian Charter of Rights and
    Freedoms, 83
capacity, 41, 44, 86, 91 n. 34, 137
  See also ability
capitalism, 29
care, 69, 70
categorical imperative, 88
Césaire, Aimé, 153
China, 21
Christman, John, 159–64, 172
coexistence, 74 n. 7
colonialism
  domination and, 18, 172
  feminism and, 27
  historical, 77
  legacies of, 85–87, 140, 154
  self-determination and, 83
colonization, 19, 20, 87
communicative action, 3
  See also *Theory of Communicative
    Action, The*
communitarianism, 41, 165
condemnation, 71
Congo, Democratic Republic of, 130
Congress, U.S., 118–19
consent, sexual, 94, 95, 141
consequentialism, 170
Constituting Critique (Goestschel), 5
contempt, 165